# LSAT®

# PrepTest 78

# Unlocked

**Exclusive Data, Analysis, & Explanations for the June 2016 LSAT**

**KAPLAN**

PUBLISHING

New York

© 2017 by Kaplan, Inc.

Published by Kaplan Publishing, a division of Kaplan, Inc.
750 Third Avenue
New York, NY 10017

ISBN: 978-1-5062-2336-0
10 9 8 7 6 5 4 3 2 1

# The Inside Story

PrepTest 78 was administered in June 2016. It challenged 23,051 test takers. What made this test so hard? Here's a breakdown of what Kaplan students who were surveyed after taking the official exam considered PrepTest 78's most difficult section.

## Hardest PrepTest 78 Section as Reported by Test Takers

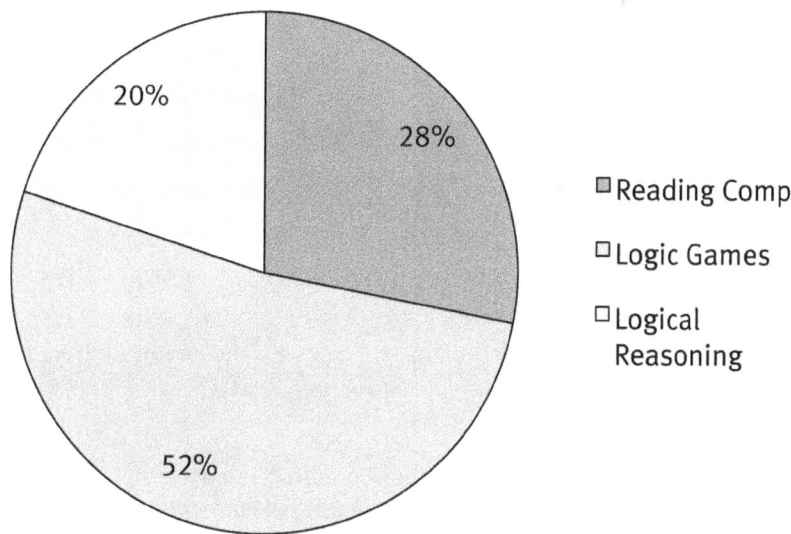

Based on these results, you might think that studying Logic Games is the key to LSAT success. Well, Logic Games is important, but test takers' perceptions don't tell the whole story. For that, you need to consider students' actual performance. The following chart shows the average number of students to miss each question in each of PrepTest 78's different sections.

# Percentage Incorrect By PrepTest 78 Section Type

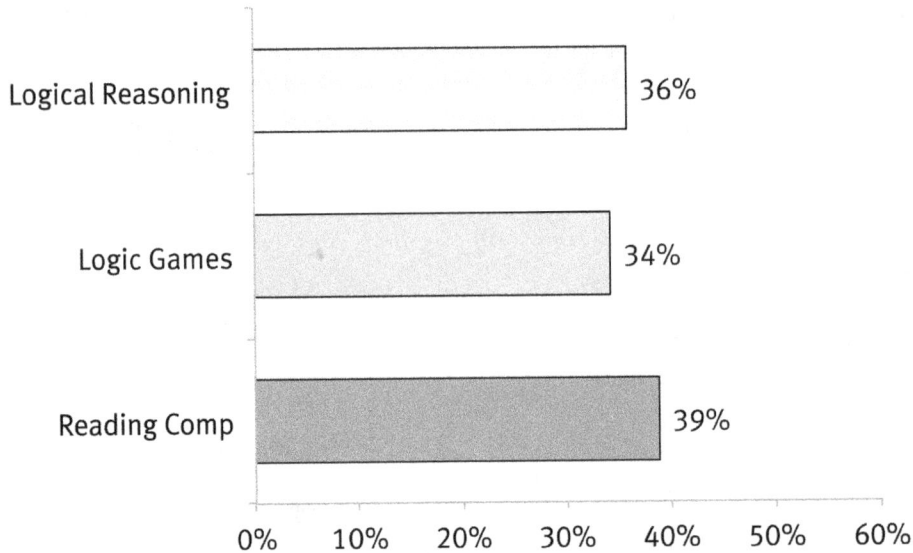

```
Logical Reasoning  |████████████████████| 36%

Logic Games        |███████████████████| 34%

Reading Comp       |█████████████████████| 39%

                   0%   10%  20%  30%  40%  50%  60%
```

Actual student performance tells quite a different story. On average, students were almost equally likely to miss questions in all three of the different section types, and on PrepTest 78, Reading Comprehension and Logical Reasoning were somewhat higher than Logic Games in actual difficulty.

Maybe students overestimate the difficulty of the Logic Games section because it's so unusual, or maybe it's because a really hard Logic Game is so easy to remember after the test. But the truth is that the test maker places hard questions throughout the test. Here were the locations of the 10 hardest (most missed) questions in the exam.

# Location of 10 Most Difficult Questions in PrepTest 78

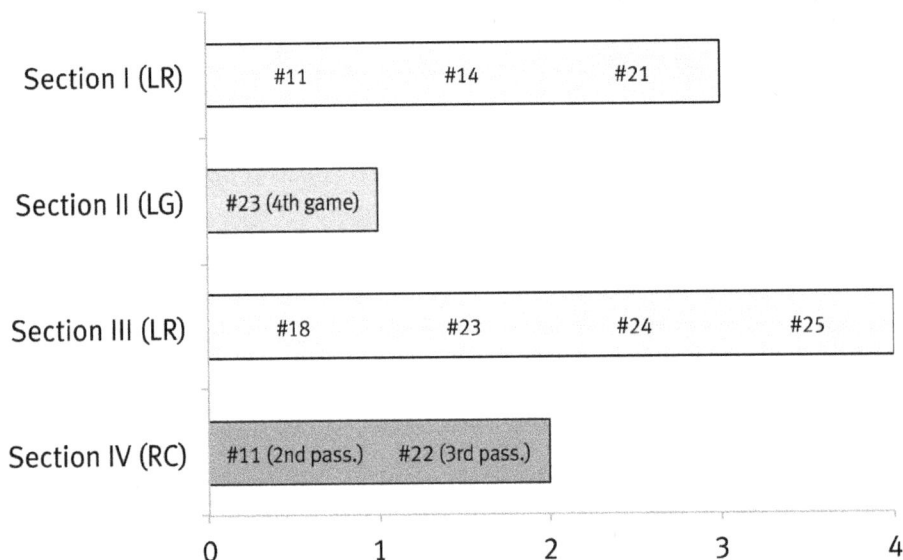

```
Section I (LR)    | #11      #14      #21          |

Section II (LG)   | #23 (4th game) |

Section III (LR)  | #18     #23     #24     #25     |

Section IV (RC)   | #11 (2nd pass.)   #22 (3rd pass.) |

                  0         1         2         3         4
```

The takeaway from this data is that, to maximize your potential on the LSAT, you need to take a comprehensive approach. Test yourself rigorously, and review your performance on every section of the test. Kaplan's LSAT explanations provide the expertise and insight you need to fully understand your results. The explanations are written and edited by a team of LSAT experts, who have helped thousands of students improve their scores. Kaplan always provides data-driven analysis of the test, ranking the difficulty of every question based on actual student performance. The ten hardest questions on every test are highlighted with a 4-star difficulty rating, the highest we give. The analysis breaks down the remaining questions into 1-, 2-, and 3-star ratings so that you can compare your performance to thousands of other test takers on all LSAC material.

Don't settle for wondering whether a question was really as hard as it seemed to you. Analyze the test with real data, and learn the secrets and strategies that help top scorers master the LSAT.

# 7 Can't-Miss Features of PrepTest 78

- Tough curve! PrepTest 78 was the first time since June '11 (PT 63) that 99 questions correct wasn't enough to get a 180.
- With only six Assumption questions and six Flaw questions, PrepTest 78 had the least combined Assumption and Flaw questions since October 2010 (PT 61).
- The Selection game returns! PrepTest 78 featured a Selection game for the first time since October '13 (PT 70) and for just the third time since 2010.
- The record for fewest Global questions in a Reading Comprehension section had been three, which had happened five times. However, on PrepTest 78, a new record was set with just two Global questions.
- The Comparative Reading pair of passages appeared in the Reading Comprehension section for the first time since December '09 (PT 59).
- Answer choices (A), (B), (C), (D), and (E) each appeared exactly 10 times in RC/LG. However, in Logical Reasoning, there was not the same consistency. In fact, (E) was twice as likely to occur as (D)—14 vs. 7 times.
- Section III kicks off with a question about unrepresentative polling. Then, less than 20 days after PrepTest 78 was administered, the United Kingdom voted for Brexit.

# PrepTest 78 in Context

As much fun as it is to find out what makes a PrepTest unique or noteworthy, it's even more important to know just how representative it is of other LSAT administrations (and, thus, how likely it is to be representative of the exam you will face on Test Day). The following charts compare the numbers of each kind of question and game on PrepTest 78 to the average numbers seen on all officially released LSATs administered over the past five years (from 2012 through 2016).

## Number of LR Questions by Type: PrepTest 78 vs. 2012–2016 Average

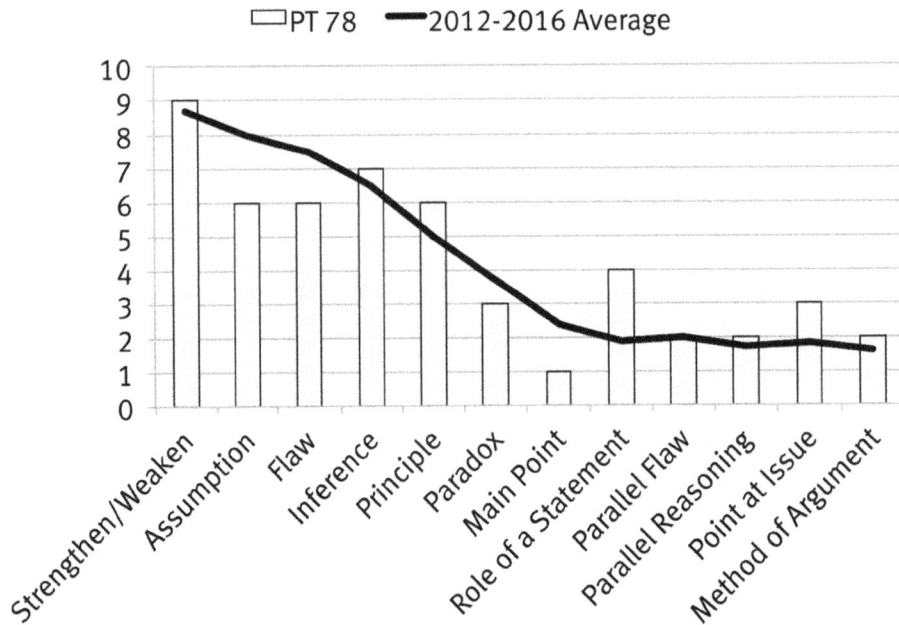

## Number of LG Games by Type: PrepTest 78 vs. 2012–2016 Average

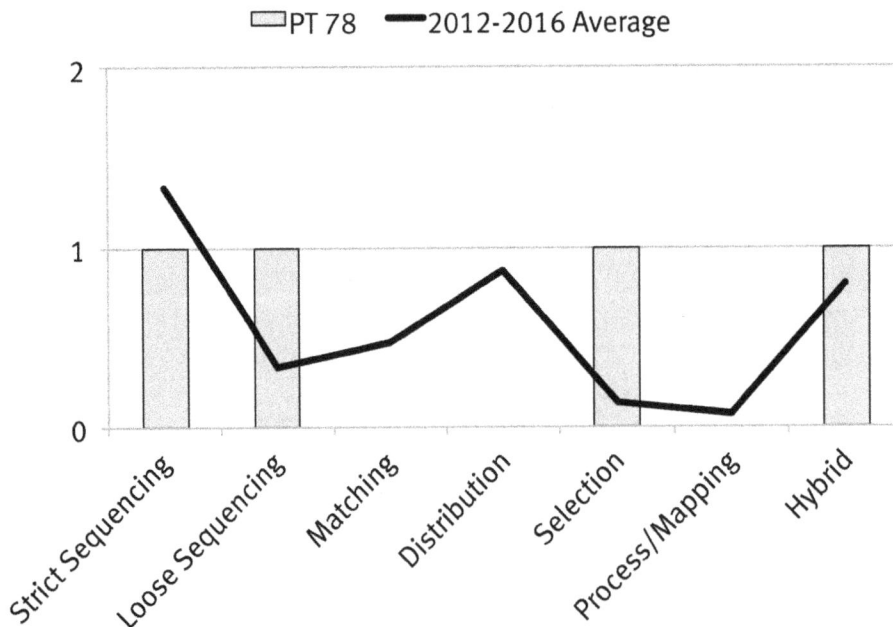

**KAPLAN**

# Number of RC Questions by Type: PrepTest 78 vs. 2012–2016 Average

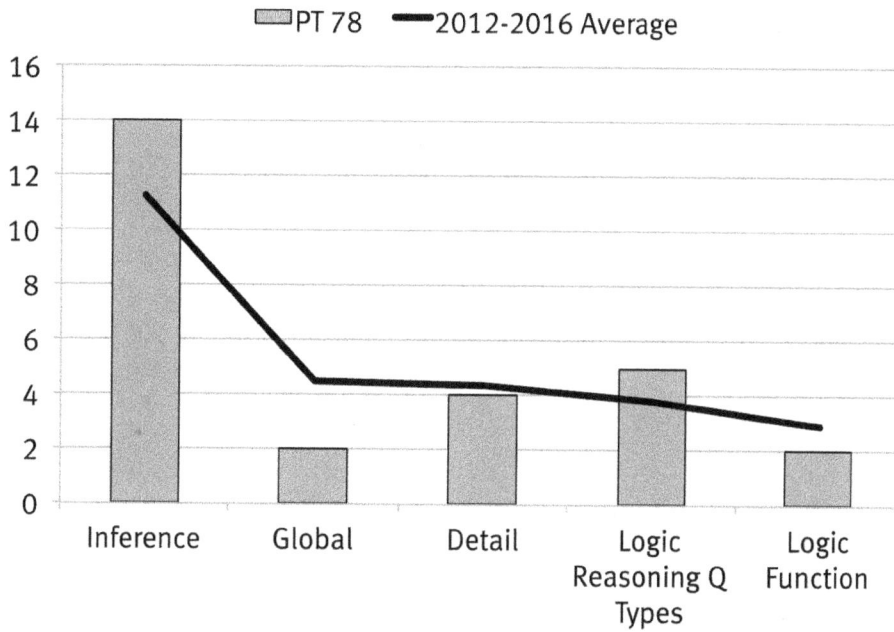

Legend: PT 78 | 2012-2016 Average

Chart: y-axis 0 to 16. Categories: Inference, Global, Detail, Logic Reasoning Q Types, Logic Function.

PT 78 bars: Inference 14, Global 2, Detail 4, Logic Reasoning Q Types ~4.8, Logic Function ~1.8.
2012-2016 Average line: Inference ~11.2, Global ~4.4, Detail ~4.3, Logic Reasoning Q Types ~3.8, Logic Function ~2.7.

There isn't usually a huge difference in the distribution of questions from LSAT to LSAT, but if this test seems harder (or easier) to you than another you've taken, compare the number of questions of the types on which you, personally, are strongest and weakest. And then, explore within each section to see if your best or worst question types came earlier or later.

Students in Kaplan's comprehensive LSAT courses have access to every released LSAT and to an online question bank with thousands of officially released questions, games, and passages. If you are studying on your own, you have to do a bit more work to identify your strengths and your areas of opportunity. Quantitative analysis (like that in the charts above) is an important tool for understanding how the test is constructed and how you are performing on it.

# Section I: Logical Reasoning

| Q# | Question Type | Correct | Difficulty |
|---|---|---|---|
| 1 | Principle (Identify/Strengthen) | A | ★ |
| 2 | Assumption (Necessary) | E | ★ |
| 3 | Method of Argument | A | ★ |
| 4 | Point at Issue | E | ★ |
| 5 | Method of Argument | B | ★ |
| 6 | Point at Issue | B | ★ |
| 7 | Flaw | B | ★ |
| 8 | Inference | C | ★★ |
| 9 | Flaw | A | ★ |
| 10 | Weaken | C | ★★ |
| 11 | Inference | A | ★★★★ |
| 12 | Strengthen | C | ★★ |
| 13 | Inference | D | ★★ |
| 14 | Assumption (Necessary) | D | ★★★★ |
| 15 | Principle (Identify/Inference) | E | ★★★ |
| 16 | Strengthen | A | ★★★ |
| 17 | Paradox | E | ★★ |
| 18 | Principle (Identify/Strengthen) | E | ★★ |
| 19 | Assumption (Necessary) | E | ★★ |
| 20 | Point at Issue | D | ★★ |
| 21 | Parallel Flaw | E | ★★★★ |
| 22 | Flaw | A | ★★ |
| 23 | Parallel Reasoning | B | ★★ |
| 24 | Principle (Identify/Assumption) | E | ★★★ |
| 25 | Weaken | C | ★ |

## 1. (A) Principle (Identify/Strengthen)

### Step 1: Identify the Question Type

The correct answer will be a broad principle that conforms to the specific content in the stimulus, making this an Identify the Principle question. Also, that principle will *justify* Hidalgo's argument, which means this Principle question will mimic a Strengthen question.

### Step 2: Untangle the Stimulus

Grecia argues that people should provide their age when responding to a particular survey. Hidalgo argues that exact ages aren't needed and that respondents should just choose from a set of age ranges.

### Step 3: Make a Prediction

Hidalgo's argument boils down to a simple recommendation: don't ask for specific ages because there's no need for that level of specificity. The correct answer will restate this in more general terms: there's no need to ask for specific information when that level of specificity is not needed.

### Step 4: Evaluate the Answer Choices

**(A)** matches the logic of Hidalgo's recommendation.

**(B)** is Out of Scope. There's no mention of how likely people are to provide *accurate* information.

**(C)** is Out of Scope. There's no mention of any "secure means of storage" for information.

**(D)** is a Distortion. Hidalgo's intention is to *prevent* the collection of *unnecessary* information. His recommendation is more of a compromise than a suggestion to collect anything that *is* needed.

**(E)** is Out of Scope. Hidalgo makes no mention of revealing anything to respondents about how information is going to be used.

## 2. (E) Assumption (Necessary)

### Step 1: Identify the Question Type

The question asks for an assumption that is *required* by the argument, making this a Necessary Assumption question.

### Step 2: Untangle the Stimulus

The author is arguing that, contrary to belief, an ancient city uncovered during excavation is not actually Troy—the legendary site of the Trojan War described in the poem the *Iliad*. As evidence, the author notes that the war lasted 10 years according to the *Iliad*, and the uncovered city was too small to survive that long a war.

### Step 3: Make a Prediction

The problem here is that the author's evidence does not come from historical records; it comes from a poem. The author overlooks the possibility that Homer may have taken some creative liberties with history. In order for this argument to work, the author must assume that the details described in the *Iliad* are accurate enough to make judgments about actual history.

### Step 4: Evaluate the Answer Choices

**(E)** must be assumed. The Denial Test confirms this. If the *Iliad* were *not* accurate about the length of the war, then the basis of the author's argument falls apart. Perhaps Homer exaggerated the length, and the uncovered city could actually be Troy. That would contradict the author, so the author must assume otherwise: the poem *was* indeed accurate.

**(A)** is irrelevant and a 180 at worst. What scholars knew in 1893 has no effect on the author's argument about the size of the city versus the length of the war. Besides, the author's argument would be stronger if this answer *weren't* true. If scholars *did* know of other potential sites for Troy, the author would have more reason to believe this city wasn't Troy.

**(B)** would help the author's cause, but is not necessary. Even if the poem *did* provide clues about the specific location, there's no indication that it would match the excavation site. And the author would still have the evidence about the size of the city and the timeline of the war.

**(C)** would also help the author's cause, but is still not necessary. No evidence of a siege would certainly support the idea that the city was not Troy. However, even if there *were* evidence of a siege, it wouldn't have to be one from the Trojan War. It could have been a minor siege, and the author's argument still stands: it was not Troy.

**(D)** is a 180. This would support the theory that the city was Troy, and the author is trying to argue it was *not* Troy.

## 3. (A) Method of Argument

### Step 1: Identify the Question Type

The word *by* indicates that the question is asking *how* Garcia responds to Flynn. That makes this a Method of Argument question. Focus on the technique Garcia uses rather than the logic behind the content.

### Step 2: Untangle the Stimulus

When dangerous products cause damage, people can sue large companies and get huge payouts. Flynn argues that this is great for consumers as it encourages companies to make products safer. Garcia disagrees, arguing that this is bad for consumers. Those lawsuits can harm companies, leading to layoffs and decreased productivity and ultimately to a weaker economy.

### Step 3: Make a Prediction

Flynn's argument in favor of big-payout lawsuits rests on one benefit. Garcia counters that by listing a series of overlooked downsides. The correct answer will describe this approach:

arguing against a point of view by raising unconsidered negatives.

**Step 4: Evaluate the Answer Choices**

**(A)** accurately describes Garcia's technique. Garcia argues that the policy Flynn supports (getting large rewards by suing corporations) has undesirable consequences (loss of jobs, a hurt economy).

**(B)** is a Distortion. Garcia attacks Flynn's *conclusion*, not one of Flynn's *premises* (i.e., his evidence). Flynn's sole premise is the incentive to reduce safety risks, and Garcia does not contradict that.

**(C)** is Out of Scope. Garcia makes no analogy to any other argument. Garcia merely points out overlooked possibilities within Flynn's argument.

**(D)** is a Distortion. Garcia shows no such self-contradiction. Garcia contradicts Flynn's argument by raising new concerns that were *not* brought up by Flynn.

**(E)** is Out of Scope. Neither Flynn nor Garcia is trying to *explain* why any particular situation occurred.

## 4. (E) Point at Issue

**Step 1: Identify the Question Type**

The stimulus provides a dialogue, and the question asks what the two speakers "disagree over." That makes this a Point at Issue question.

**Step 2: Untangle the Stimulus**

Monroe argues that a project, designed to cut back as much as possible the number of homes without electricity, was a failure. As evidence, Monroe cites 2,000 homes that are still without electricity. Wilkerson counters that the project was a success because it did bring electricity to 3,000 homes that didn't have any.

**Step 3: Make a Prediction**

Simply put, Monroe and Wilkerson disagree over whether the project was a success or a failure. Furthermore, this disagreement is based on how each author interprets the "2,000 homes" statistic. So, Monroe and Wilkerson are arguing over whether those 2,000 homes represent a success or a failure.

**Step 4: Evaluate the Answer Choices**

**(E)** is the point at issue. Monroe argues that the 2,000 homes without electricity *does* count as a failure, while Wilkerson argues that it does *not*—it's actually a success!

**(A)** is a 180. Monroe and Wilkerson *agree* about the number of homes left without electricity. What they disagree about is whether that number constitutes a success or a failure for the project.

**(B)** is not a point at issue. Monroe doesn't address the number of homes without electricity *before* the project began. In all likelihood, Monroe would agree with Wilkerson about that figure. The real issue about the success of the project revolves around the number of houses left without electricity *afterward*.

**(C)** is Extreme. Monroe's assessment of the project's failure is based on a substantial number of homes without electricity: 2,000. There's no evidence that Monroe would consider the project a failure at *any* number. It's possible that Monroe just has a threshold for homes still without electricity (say, 100 homes or less), but 2,000 homes was just too much.

**(D)** is not a point at issue. Monroe brings up this stated goal, but Wilkerson never disputes it. The point at issue is whether or not the project *met* that goal.

## 5. (B) Method of Argument

**Step 1: Identify the Question Type**

The word *by* indicates that the answer will describe *how* the author weakens a conclusion drawn by someone else. That makes this a Method of Argument question.

**Step 2: Untangle the Stimulus**

Researchers surveyed an equal number of 20-year-olds and 50-year-olds about donating blood. Because more 50-year-olds claimed to give blood, the researchers concluded that 50-year-olds are more altruistic. The author disagrees, suggesting that some people may misrepresent their behavior if they feel it doesn't live up to societal expectations.

**Step 3: Make a Prediction**

Basically, the author is suggesting that some of those seemingly altruistic 50-year-olds are just a bunch of liars, unwilling to admit that they're not the generous donators they're expected to be. In short, the author questions the researcher's conclusion by taking a more cynical interpretation of the survey results.

**Step 4: Evaluate the Answer Choices**

**(B)** matches the author's technique. The author uses the same data, but offers an alternative explanation (they're not more altruistic—they're just trying to make themselves look good!).

**(A)** is Out of Scope. The author never questions the sample group selected. The author just questions their motives in answering the survey question.

**(C)** is Out of Scope. The author's argument is based on people's motives when answering the survey question. The author never mentions direct observation of altruistic acts.

**(D)** is a Distortion. The author criticizes the motives of the people *responding* to the survey, not the researchers administering the survey.

**(E)** is Out of Scope. The author only makes general claims about "[m]any people." No specific examples are given.

## 6. (B) Point at Issue

### Step 1: Identify the Question Type

This is a Dialogue/Response stimulus, and the question asks for something the speakers "disagree over." That makes this a Point at Issue question.

### Step 2: Untangle the Stimulus

The only rug store in Glendale just went out of business. According to Mario, this indicates low demand for rugs in Glendale, so opening a new rug business there would be a bad idea. Renate disagrees, suggesting demand for the product is not an issue. One place closing just opens the market up for a new rug store.

### Step 3: Make a Prediction

To Mario, the rug market is dead. Renate says quite the opposite: with a wide open market, now is probably a great time to open a new rug store. So, their primary disagreement is about whether opening a new rug store is a good idea or not.

### Step 4: Evaluate the Answer Choices

**(B)** is the point at issue. Mario says it's not a good idea ("rugs would be one product to avoid"), while Renate suggest it *is* a good idea ("the market for rugs . . . is now wide open").

**(A)** is Out of Scope. Neither Mario nor Renate address the quality of the rugs.

**(C)** is either Out of Scope or potentially a 180. Neither speaker talks about whether it's possible to determine the market for rugs. However, because Mario and Renate both make judgments about the rug market, this suggests that they agree that it is possible to determine the market. They just disagree on the size of the market.

**(D)** is Out of Scope. Neither speaker mentions any other stores going out of business.

**(E)** is a Distortion. Mario clearly agrees that low demand can lead to a rug store closing. While Renate does not feel that low demand was the problem for the store in Glendale, that's not to say that low demand couldn't be the cause for other rug stores closing. Renate's opinion on this statement cannot be determined, so it cannot be the point at issue.

## 7. (B) Flaw

### Step 1: Identify the Question Type

The question directly asks for the flaw in the argument.

### Step 2: Untangle the Stimulus

The city council claims that the latest technology would prevent safety issues that could arise from expanding the airport's air traffic beyond its original capacity. The editorialist argues otherwise: the technology would *not* prevent safety issues. As evidence, the editorialist cites studies that show the latest technology does nothing to prevent safety issues.

### Step 3: Make a Prediction

Unfortunately, the editorialist refers to studies from *30 years ago*. Technology could have changed drastically over that time, and it's possible that *today's* technology could prevent a decrease in safety far better than anything from 30 years ago. The editorialist completely overlooks this, and that is the flaw.

### Step 4: Evaluate the Answer Choices

**(B)** accurately describes the flaw. The editorialist fails to consider that safety depends on what the latest technology is, assuming that what was true of the latest technology 30 years ago still holds true with today's technology.

**(A)** is inaccurate. The conclusion is based on "numerous studies," not a general statement. And those studies reflected what would happen at "every airport," not just a few specific instances.

**(C)** is Out of Scope. It doesn't matter whether or not the council was aware of the old studies. The editorialist's mistake is using those potentially outdated studies as evidence in the first place.

**(D)** is not accurate. There is no absence of evidence for the claim of safety. The council provides evidence: the airport would use the latest technology.

**(E)** is Out of Scope. This argument is entirely about whether safety would decrease or not. There's no judgment about whether this is *acceptable* or not based on other non-safety benefits.

## 8. (C) Inference

### Step 1: Identify the Question Type

It is difficult to categorize this question by the stem alone. What fills in the blank at the end of an argument depends on what surrounds the blank. In this case, the blank completes a train of thought that is supported by everything before it. That makes it an Inference question. It could also arguably be considered a Sufficient Assumption question, but the stimulus will help you see that the argument is basically already complete; you just have to infer what completes the analogy.

### Step 2: Untangle the Stimulus

Some people claim that the existence of different moral codes shows that morality is developed through culture and is not universally part of our nature. The philosopher disagrees, citing particular shared moral attitudes. The philosopher then makes an analogy to food, saying that all people share tastes but can still have different cuisines.

### Step 3: Make a Prediction

The phrase "[t]his argument is flawed" is important. The philosopher argues that, despite what people say, there *could* be some universal grounds for morality even though different cultures have different moral codes. However, the philosopher never directly states this, so it will likely fill in the blank at the end. In addition, the blank comes at the end of an analogy. So, the phrasing of the philosopher's view will conform to the logic of the analogy. For food, different cultures may have different cuisines, but those cuisines are still based on shared/universal tastes (e.g., sweetness). This compares perfectly to the philosopher's point: different cultures may have different moral codes, but those codes are still based on shared/universal moral attitudes (e.g., cruelty is wrong).

### Step 4: Evaluate the Answer Choices

**(C)** matches the philosopher's point about shared moral attitudes despite differing moral codes.

**(A)** is a 180. It has been argued that moral codes are a product of culture (i.e., they're based on where they arise), but the philosopher is arguing against that, saying such reasoning is *flawed*.

**(B)** is a Distortion and Extreme. While there may be some resemblance among moral codes, this does not match the analogy that shared traits (tastes) can "provide the basis" for different large-scale ideas (cuisines). Nothing indicates that *most* cuisines resemble each other, so it would be too much to say the moral codes of *most* cultures resemble each other.

**(D)** is Out of Scope. The philosopher is not discussing whether *understanding* the basis of moral codes is possible or not.

**(E)** is a Distortion. The philosopher is trying to argue that universal shared moral attitudes exist, not that these moral attitudes can be changed to fit a moral code.

### 9. (A) Flaw

#### Step 1: Identify the Question Type

The question asks why the argument is "vulnerable to criticism," which means it is asking for the flaw in the argument.

#### Step 2: Untangle the Stimulus

The author concludes (as indicated by the word [*t*]*hus*) that more plant species make prairies better able to support plants. As evidence, the author cites a study in which prairies with more plant species had healthier plants and more nutrient-rich soil.

### Step 3: Make a Prediction

This is one of the most common flaws tested on the LSAT. The evidence describes a correlation (the data lines up: more plant species correlates with plant and soil quality). The author then concludes one thing caused the other (more species was the cause of the prairie's great growing conditions). There are three flaws in this case: 1) the author overlooks alternative causes (i.e., something else could have led to great growing conditions), 2) the causality could be reversed (i.e., the quality of the prairie is responsible for the greater number of species), and 3) it could just be a coincidence. The correct answer will identify one of these three flaws.

### Step 4: Evaluate the Answer Choices

**(A)** describes one of the common flaws in causal arguments, just in algebraic terms. Replacing X with "more plant species" and Y with "better ability to support plants," this basically says more species caused the better plant support when the causality could be reversed (better plant support could have caused more species).

**(B)** is irrelevant. The author doesn't need to describe a specific mechanism to claim that one thing led to another.

**(C)** is a Distortion. The author never uses characteristics of one particular plot. The author uses data about prairie plots in general.

**(D)** is unsupported. The data is said to come from a "study of prairie plants." There's no indication that the sample size or population was unrepresentative.

**(E)** is Out of Scope. The author makes no claim about proportions.

### 10. (C) Weaken

#### Step 1: Identify the Question Type

This question directly asks for something that weakens the given argument.

#### Step 2: Untangle the Stimulus

The anthropologist describes an experiment in which two groups of students were taught how to make a Neanderthal tool. One group was taught visually and verbally, while the other group was given no oral instruction. Both groups learned equally well. So, the anthropologist concludes that Neanderthals didn't need language to make their sophisticated tools.

#### Step 3: Make a Prediction

The conclusion brings up *sophisticated* tools. However, the study doesn't say the students were asked to make sophisticated tools. They were just shown how to create "one of the types" of tools Neanderthals made. Maybe they learned to make a tool that was absurdly simplistic. In that case, Neanderthals may have needed language for the more sophisticated tools, raising considerable doubts about the anthropologist's claim.

**Step 4: Evaluate the Answer Choices**

**(C)** attacks the anthropologist's assumption about the tools created by the undergrads. If they made simplistic tools, then the author has no evidence to back up a claim about sophisticated tools—and the argument falls apart.

**(A)** has no effect on the anthropologist's argument. The argument is not about whether or not Neanderthals actually had language, but whether or not they could make their tools even "if they had no language."

**(B)** is a 180. If members of the second group couldn't even talk to one another and still performed equally well, the anthropologist's claim that language is unnecessary would be *strengthened*.

**(D)** is an Irrelevant Comparison at best and a 180 at worst. The proficiency of the instructors does not change the results. Even if it did have some effect, the silent group *still* did just as well with an inferior teacher. This could only reinforce the fact that language is really not necessary.

**(E)** is an Irrelevant Comparison. If the Neanderthal tools were less sophisticated, then it's still possible that language wasn't needed to create those tools (as the anthropologist claims). So, bringing up evidence about another group does not weaken the argument.

## 11. (A) Inference

**Step 1: Identify the Question Type**

The correct answer will be "supported by" the information given, which means this is an Inference question.

**Step 2: Untangle the Stimulus**

The author presents information about exercising to improve one's cardiovascular health. One *can* see dramatic results with moderate exercise, e.g., half an hour of walking most days of the week. Sure, one could get even *more* results from more strenuous exercise, but that's not really needed.

**Step 3: Make a Prediction**

It's difficult to predict exactly what the correct answer will say, but it will be consistent with the information provided: modest exercise may be good enough to help dramatically improve cardiovascular health; you could do more, but you don't need to.

**Step 4: Evaluate the Answer Choices**

**(A)** is supported. The author does claim that even modest exercise on most days can produce improvement. And if "more vigorous exercise is more effective," then strenuous

exercise on most days could also certainly help—even if it's not absolutely necessary.

**(B)** is a Distortion. The author claims that half an hour of walking most days of the week (i.e., at least four days a week, which would be at least two hours of walking) can help. This suggests that you can take the same amount of hours and condense it into two or three days. However, the author never suggests you can do that. Instead, the author states "one should exercise most days," which means one may not get the same results by spacing things out too much. Furthermore, the first sentence says that modest exercise *can* produce improvements in cardiovascular health. However, that is a lower level of certainty than saying it *generally* produces dramatic improvements.

**(C)** is a 180. Even though strenuous exercise is not necessary, the author directly says that more vigorous (i.e., strenuous) exercise would still be "more effective" than modest exercise.

**(D)** is Extreme. The author only discusses exercise and does not exclude other ways to improve cardiovascular health.

**(E)** is a 180, directly contradicting the last sentence which claims "a strenuous workout is not absolutely necessary."

## 12. (C) Strengthen

**Step 1: Identify the Question Type**

The question directly asks for something that strengthens the given argument.

**Step 2: Untangle the Stimulus**

The author concludes that Sartore is a better movie reviewer than Kelly. The evidence is that reviews should help people determine if they're likely to enjoy a movie or not, and when people realize they're likely to enjoy a particular movie, that is more likely to come from one of Sartore's reviews.

**Step 3: Make a Prediction**

The goal of a review is to help readers determine whether they're likely to enjoy a movie *or not*. The evidence only talks about Sartore's ability to help people recognize movies they *are* likely to enjoy. The author assumes that this means Sartore's reviews also help people recognize movies they are *not* likely to enjoy. The correct answer will validate this.

**Step 4: Evaluate the Answer Choices**

**(C)** strengthens the argument by looking at both goals of a movie review. Now, Sartore's reviews better help people recognize when they're likely to enjoy a movie and when they're *not* likely to.

**(A)** may be a tempting answer, as many people might feel technical knowledge makes one a better movie critic. However, this author's judgment is based on the reviewer's ability to help people recognize what movies they are likely to enjoy. The comparison between technical knowledge and fandom cannot be absolutely connected to that ability. At worst, some could argue that people are more likely to be persuaded by a movie fan than some stuffy technical analyst.

**(B)** is irrelevant. The proportion of favorable versus unfavorable reviews does nothing to indicate whether readers are influenced by these reviews or not. If Sartore is better able to help people identify if they enjoy a movie or not, then the quantity of negative and positive reviews is immaterial.

**(D)** is irrelevant. The argument is not based on how much readers *actually* enjoy the movie. It's based on whether the review helps them realize whether or not they're *likely* to enjoy the movie. The point of the review is not to make one enjoy the movie *more*; the point is to better ascertain which movies are worth watching and which ones are worth avoiding.

**(E)** is an Irrelevant Comparison. It doesn't matter how many movies they review in common. All that matters is their ability to influence readers.

### 13. (D) Inference

**Step 1: Identify the Question Type**

The correct answer will be "strongly supported by the information" provided, which means it will be a logical inference.

**Step 2: Untangle the Stimulus**

The author discusses specially bred fish. Their colors and unique shapes make them appealing, but there are downsides. Their shape slows them down at feeding time, so they won't eat enough when they're competing against faster ordinary fish. And when they breed, their offspring aren't as colorful or uniquely shaped.

**Step 3: Make a Prediction**

There are many possible inferences here, so just take time to consider the major details. The author provides various pros (colorful, interesting shapes) and cons (slow, dull offspring) of specially bred fish. They are also compared to ordinary fish. Specially bred fish are inferior, and they move more slowly due to their body shapes. Watch out for answers that are too strong or bring up concepts not addressed in the stimulus.

**Step 4: Evaluate the Answer Choices**

**(D)** is supported. Ordinary fish are said to reach food more quickly because the specially bred ones are "[h]ampered by their elaborate tails or strangely shaped fins." That directly suggests that ordinary fish lack those drawbacks.

**(A)** is Extreme. Special care would probably be recommended, but the stimulus merely says that specially bred fish are *often* underfed. That suggests they *could* do okay without special care. Special care is not described as a *must*.

**(B)** is unsupported. While specially bred fish are said to be "popular with connoisseurs," that doesn't mean other fish are not popular. Connoisseurs could very well like ordinary fish, too.

**(C)** is Extreme. Specially bred fish may be *popular* with connoisseurs, but that doesn't mean *most* of these fish are bought by connoisseurs.

**(E)** is a 180. The offspring may not be as unique, but there *are* offspring. There is no reproductive interference.

### 14. (D) Assumption (Necessary)

**Step 1: Identify the Question Type**

The question directly asks for an assumption, and one that is *required* by the argument. That makes this a Necessary Assumption question.

**Step 2: Untangle the Stimulus**

The ethicist concludes that the principle "if one ought to do something, then one can do it" is not always true. In other words, we can't always do what we should. As evidence, the ethicist provides an example of someone unable to fulfill a promise due to unexpected traffic.

**Step 3: Make a Prediction**

The ethicist argues that we can't always do what we *ought to* based on an example showing that we can't always keep our *promises*. That leads to the basic assumption that we ought to do what we promise.

> *If*    *promise something*  →    *ought to do it*

That seems reasonable, but the ethicist makes this assumption in a situation in which the promise is *impossible* to keep. So, the ethicist must assume that an *impossible* promise is still a promise, and one still ought to do what is promised. And given that there are promises that are impossible to keep, the general principle that "if one ought to, then one can" does not always hold.

**Step 4: Evaluate the Answer Choices**

**(D)** must be assumed. This confirms that one ought to keep (i.e., is obligated to complete) any promise, even when that promise cannot be kept.

**(A)** reverses the logic of the necessary assumption. The Formal Logic here states that "if something ought to have been done, then it was promised."

> *If*    *ought*    →    *promise*

However, the ethicist's assumption goes the other way: "if something is promised, then it is something that ought to be done."

> *If*    *promise*    →    *ought*

The part about *failing* doesn't cause the terms to be negated. Failing to deliver on a promise is not the same as "not promising," and failing to do what ought to be done isn't the same as "ought not to do it."

**(B)** is a 180. The ethicist assumes that events like traffic jams do *not* excuse people from the obligation. It's still something they ought to do, even if they can't.

**(C)** is Out of Scope. This argument is about what people *should* do, not what they *shouldn't*.

**(E)** is Out of Scope. The ethicist does not question whether people should *make* promises, but whether people ought to *keep* those promises—even when they become impossible.

## 15. (E) Principle (Identify/Inference)

### Step 1: Identify the Question Type

The correct answer will be a *generalization* to which the given situation conforms. That makes this an Identify the Principle question. Because the stimulus is described as a *situation*, don't look for evidence and a conclusion. Just consider what happens, and look for an answer that matches the facts, just like you would in an Inference question, but in broader terms.

### Step 2: Untangle the Stimulus

As leather and fur have become less fashionable, their prices have dropped. Other materials, which are now more fashionable, have risen in price. This is despite the fact that leather and fur require more intensive labor than the new fashionable materials.

### Step 3: Make a Prediction

With both sets of materials, the prices are correlated with fashion trends. It doesn't matter that leather and fur require more labor to make. So, as a general rule, it appears that the price of materials is driven by more than just labor costs.

### Step 4: Evaluate the Answer Choices

**(E)** matches the logic. Fashion trends have moved away from leather and fur and toward other materials, and the prices of both groups have adjusted accordingly.

**(A)** is Out of Scope. The stimulus only provides information about the price of raw materials (e.g., leather and fur), not the final price of manufactured goods. Furthermore, even though fashion trends certainly influence the overall price of a material, it is not clear that they influence the price *more* than the cost of producing the materials. Prices have been adjusted based on fashion trends, but perhaps labor costs still play the most important role.

**(B)** is Out of Scope. The stimulus mentions nothing about the practicality of the materials.

**(C)** is a Distortion. While materials requiring little labor are becoming more fashionable *now*, labor-intensive leather and fur *were* fashionable at one point. And there's always a

chance fashion can change and return to something more labor-intensive.

**(D)** is Out of Scope. The stimulus never mentions the appearance of the final manufactured good, and never discusses what makes something fashionable.

## 16. (A) Strengthen

### Step 1: Identify the Question Type

Fill-in-the-blank questions cannot always be classified simply by the existence of the blank; they also depend on the Keywords in the stimulus. This question stem directly mentions that what fills in the blank will "strongly support" the argument's conclusion, which indicates a Strengthen question. The blank also concludes a sentence beginning with "[a]fter all," which indicates evidence. So, the blank could also be considered an unstated piece of evidence that completes the argument, which would make this a Sufficient Assumption question. Either way, the correct answer will create a stronger connection between the given evidence and the conclusion.

### Step 2: Untangle the Stimulus

The author concludes that an outbreak of certain moths in most of the forest should not be stopped. As evidence, the author cites that the moths help in areas where the forest is crowded with immature trees.

### Step 3: Make a Prediction

The author wants to keep the moths around because they are beneficial . . . when the forest is crowded with immature trees. However, there's no evidence that this is the case in the forest mentioned. The author just assumes it is. The correct answer will verify that *most* of the forest in discussion is crowded with immature trees.

### Step 4: Evaluate the Answer Choices

**(A)** backs up the conclusion. If most of the forest is crowded with immature trees, then it is warranted to keep the moths around for the benefit they provide.

**(B)** is potentially a 180. If the forest only has a few immature trees and many mature trees, then this could pose a major problem. The moths are only said to be beneficial when a forest is overcrowded with immature trees. However, if the moths eat mature trees first, they won't impact how crowded the forest is with immature trees, and they could destroy a significant number of mature trees first.

**(C)** is an Irrelevant Comparison. Which trees are more often affected by forest fires has no bearing on whether the forest in question meets the conditions that would warrant keeping the moths around.

**(D)** does not help. This makes the outbreak more likely to happen, but still does not validate that it's a good idea for the forest in question.

**(E)** is irrelevant. The author doesn't want to use any countermeasures, so their effectiveness has no bearing on the argument.

## 17. (E) Paradox

### Step 1: Identify the Question Type

The question asks for something that would *explain* the statistics provided. That makes this a Paradox question.

### Step 2: Untangle the Stimulus

The city of Gastner just built a new highway to reduce traffic, but travel times in the city actually got *worse* after the new highway opened.

### Step 3: Make a Prediction

Paradox questions contain a central mystery. In this case, why did commute times get *longer* when the highway was supposed to help? Something must have happened to offset the time savings granted by the new highway. There could be several options, so don't predict anything specific. Just look for an answer that mentions a side effect that would somehow create *more* traffic.

### Step 4: Evaluate the Answer Choices

**(E)** provides an explanation. While the highway may have reduced traffic from the suburbs to the downtown area, it caused *more* traffic *in* the downtown area. Perhaps more people were willing to drive into downtown after completion of the new highway. So, people got to the city faster only to hit more traffic once they got there.

**(A)** is irrelevant. The new highway provided new links to the suburbs, so it should have helped by giving people additional options into the city. This doesn't explain why things got worse.

**(B)** is also irrelevant. Even if the new highway were only convenient for certain people, it still should have helped *them*, indirectly reducing the number of people on other roads.

**(C)** is a 180. This says the suburban roads were *upgraded*, which suggests improvement. That doesn't help explain why things got worse.

**(D)** is irrelevant. The mystery is about the increase in travel time *after* the highway opened. Roadwork that occurred during construction (i.e., *before* it opened) doesn't help explain anything.

## 18. (E) Principle (Identify/Strengthen)

### Step 1: Identify the Question Type

The question directly asks for a principle, and one that will *justify* the given reasoning. That makes it an Identify the Principle question that mimics a Strengthen question.

### Step 2: Untangle the Stimulus

The office worker has two unfinished projects and argues for working exclusively on the second project. The first one is already late, and working more on the first one would make it impossible to finish the second one on time.

### Step 3: Make a Prediction

Both projects are equally important, so that has no bearing on the decision. The decision comes down to two options: 1) keep working on the already late project, and make both projects late, or 2) work on the other project, and at least have a chance of getting one project done on time. By choosing the second option, the office worker is acting on the principle that it's better to try getting *something* done on time instead of being late with everything.

### Step 4: Evaluate the Answer Choices

**(E)** validates the office worker's logic. The office worker argues in favor of the second project (a project that could be finished on time) over the first project (a late project of equal priority).

**(A)** does not help. This fits the idea of devoting time exclusively to one project, but gives no justification for choosing the second project over the first.

**(B)** is a Distortion. The office worker is not concerned about failing to finish either project. The office worker is merely concerned about finishing the projects *on time*.

**(C)** is Out of Scope. Both projects are said to be "equally important." There's no suggestion that one "must be done" while the other is "merely optional."

**(D)** is Out of Scope. The office worker makes no mention of worries or the prospect of those worries interfering with the projects.

## 19. (E) Assumption (Necessary)

### Step 1: Identify the Question Type

The question asks for an assumption that the argument *requires*, making this a Necessary Assumption question.

### Step 2: Untangle the Stimulus

The science teacher concludes ([*t*]*herefore*) that science courses should teach evaluation of science-based arguments regarding practical issues rather than just abstract concepts. As evidence, the teacher claims that courses should teach skills useful in everyday life, and abstract concepts are rarely useful.

## Step 3: Make a Prediction

The science teacher mentions that abstract concepts are not useful, but never actually states that evaluation of science-based arguments regarding practical issues *is* useful. The teacher must assume such evaluation is useful in everyday life, otherwise there'd be no reason to recommend it over abstract concepts.

## Step 4: Evaluate the Answer Choices

**(E)** must be true. The science teacher's argument rests entirely on teaching skills that are useful. Using the Denial Test, if the ability to evaluate arguments were *not* useful in everyday life, then there would be no reason to recommend it. The teacher's argument would fall apart. So, the teacher must assume it can be useful.

**(A)** is Extreme and even a 180. The science teacher does not claim that useful skills are the *only* things that should be taught. In fact, the teacher claims in the very last line that the useful skills could be taught "in addition to" abstract aspects, which the teacher already cited as "very seldom useful."

**(B)** is a 180. The science teacher favors argument evaluation of practical issues more than abstract aspects. In fact, the teacher argues it would be okay to teach evaluation "instead of" abstract concepts.

**(C)** is an Irrelevant Comparison. It doesn't matter who would be better at learning argument evaluation. The argument is only concerned with teaching it in the first place.

**(D)** is Out of Scope and Extreme. The argument is about what *should* be done, not what *is* or *is not* being done. Furthermore, putting **(D)** to the Denial Test would give a negated answer of "*some* secondary school science courses *do* currently teach students to evaluate arguments regarding practical issues." The existence of some schools that are already compliant with the recommendation would hardly destroy the science teacher's argument.

## 20. (D) Point at Issue

### Step 1: Identify the Question Type

The question asks for a "point of disagreement" between two speakers, making this a Point at Issue question.

### Step 2: Untangle the Stimulus

Lyle concludes that modernizing the language of old plays helps teach history. This is because modernization makes the play more accessible, even if it affects the aesthetic quality. Carl concludes ([*t*]*hus*) that modernizing language is of *no use* to teaching history. This is because it prevents full understanding, making it impossible to get a deep knowledge of the past.

## Step 3: Make a Prediction

The point at issue is fairly transparent as Lyle says modernizing language is "valuable for teaching history," and Carl says it is "of no use for teaching history." Neither speaker addresses the other's evidence, so disagreement there cannot be discerned. The correct answer will stick to the core issue: whether modernizing language is valuable for teaching history.

## Step 4: Evaluate the Answer Choices

**(D)** is the point at issue. Lyle says such modernizing *is* valuable, while Carl says it is decidedly *not*.

**(A)** is Out of Scope. Neither speaker assesses the pedagogical value of the original play. They only address the value of the modernization. If anything, they would probably *agree* that the value is *different*. The real issue is whether that difference is positive or not.

**(B)** is a Distortion. Both speakers are concerned with the effect of modernized language, not the loss of aesthetic quality. If anything, Lyle finds the lessened aesthetic quality irrelevant while Carl offers no opinion whatsoever about the loss of aesthetic quality.

**(C)** is Out of Scope. Neither speaker is concerned about what would be *most* aesthetically enjoyable.

**(E)** is a Distortion. Lyle makes this suggestion, but Carl expresses no opinion about aesthetic qualities or loss thereof.

## 21. (E) Parallel Flaw

### Step 1: Identify the Question Type

The correct answer will be an argument that is "parallel to" the one in the stimulus, which is described as *flawed*. That makes this a Parallel Flaw question. The correct answer must commit the exact same flaw as the argument in the stimulus.

### Step 2: Untangle the Stimulus

The stimulus's author concludes that some soils contain clay and sand while other soils contain clay and organic material. This is because most soil contains clay, and almost all soil has sand or organic material.

### Step 3: Make a Prediction

The problem here is that almost all soil contains sand *or* organic material. However, it's impossible to tell which one is more common. It's possible that 90% of soil has sand while only 9% has organic material (for a total of 99%—virtually all soil having one or the other), yet clay might only appear in soil with sand (90%—still most soil). Based on the two overlapping majorities, clay will certainly appear with sand *or* organic material, but there's no guarantee it will appear with sand in some soils *and* with organic materials in others, as the original argument concludes. The correct answer will make the same flawed shift from *or* to *and*. It might be helpful to set up an algebraic formula to compare the logic. The evidence is that most items (soils) have X (clay), and almost all of those items have Y *or* Z (sand or organic materials). The conclusion is that some items have X and Y *and* others have X and Z.

### Step 4: Evaluate the Answer Choices

**(E)** matches the flawed logic. The evidence is that most items (pharmacies) have X (cosmetics), and almost all those items have Y or Z (shampoo or toothpaste). The conclusion is that some items have X and Y *and* others have X and Z. Like the original, it's possible that 90% of pharmacies have shampoo and 9% have toothpaste, and cosmetics could be sold only where shampoo is sold. There's no guarantee it would also be sold with toothpaste.

**(A)** has perfect evidence. However, the conclusion is conditional, based solely on *if* cosmetics are sold with toothpaste. If cosmetics are sold with shampoo, the conclusion doesn't trigger anything. So, the conclusion leaves open the door that cosmetics could be sold without toothpaste, taking away part of the original's flaw.

**(B)** mixes up the evidence and conclusion, concluding that most pharmacies sell cosmetics based on evidence of what *some* pharmacies sell. A conclusion about *most* pharmacies cannot be drawn from evidence about *some* pharmacies, but that's not the same flaw as the original.

**(C)** matches the evidence. However, the conclusion here is actually logical, not flawed. This is saying that if there's no pharmacy with cosmetics and toothpaste, then there must be some with cosmetics and shampoo. In other words, there must be pharmacies with at least cosmetics and toothpaste *or* cosmetics and shampoo, not necessarily both. This properly retains the *or* in the logic from evidence to conclusion.

**(D)** has the correct conclusion, but it is based on different evidence, and thus does not match. Instead of evidence that almost all pharmacies have Y or Z (shampoo or toothpaste), the evidence here is that almost all pharmacies with Y *also* have Z. That ignores all the pharmacies that *don't* have Y—a flaw not found in the original argument.

## 22. (A) Flaw

### Step 1: Identify the Question Type

The question asks why the argument given is "vulnerable to criticism," which means it is asking for the flaw in the reasoning.

### Step 2: Untangle the Stimulus

The author concludes that PCB regulation effectively reduced exposure to PCBs based on a study showing that younger test subjects had lower levels of PCBs.

### Step 3: Make a Prediction

The author wisely addresses representativeness issues by admitting that "valid inferences could not be drawn from the study because of the small sample size." And yet, just two sentences later, the author claims that the study *proves* that regulations were effective. So, the flaw is the author's insistence that a conclusion is *proven* based on a study the author outright admitted could not be used to infer anything.

### Step 4: Evaluate the Answer Choices

**(A)** identifies the flaw. This inconsistency is apparent when the author claims "inferences could not be drawn from the study" and then proceeds to draw an inference from the study.

**(B)** is Out of Scope. The author is only concerned about PCB levels, not other chemicals or any effects.

**(C)** is Out of Scope. The evidence never mentions any lack of evidence against the PCB regulations.

**(D)** is not applicable here. While claims of causality can sometimes confuse cause and effect, there's no reason to suggest that the author is doing that here. This answer suggests that the PCB-banning regulation could have been an *effect* (rather than the *cause*) of reduced PCB levels—but that doesn't make sense.

**(E)** is Out of Scope. The argument is only about exposure to PCBs, not the effects.

## 23. (B) Parallel Reasoning

### Step 1: Identify the Question Type

The correct answer will be an argument that is "similar in its reasoning" to the given argument. That makes this a Parallel Reasoning question.

### Step 2: Untangle the Stimulus

The author presents a discrepancy in learning about spies: we can learn a lot about why they fail, but much less about why they succeed. This is because spies generally don't reveal their methods unless they fail (i.e., are caught).

### Step 3: Make a Prediction

The argument is based on how limited evidence can lead to lopsided information. If information is mostly limited to failures, then it makes sense that that's what we learn the most about. The correct answer will present similar results on a different topic: information will be mainly limited to one side of a situation, so that is what we mostly learn about.

### Step 4: Evaluate the Answer Choices

**(B)** is a match. Information about motives is mainly limited to one side (motives people are aware of), so that is what we mostly learn about.

**(A)** draws a conclusion about a requirement and makes no mention of a situation in which we learn more about one side than another. Furthermore, the stimulus is limited to spies who were caught and those who were not, but **(A)** contains three groups of people: those who succeeded at the marathon, those who failed, and those who did not participate.

**(C)** concludes that something is unclear and provides a condition that would have provided more clarity. Not only does that not match the original logic, but it fails to mention how we learn more about one aspect of a situation over another.

**(D)** does not compare one side of a situation to another. Instead, it just describes how one category of people is already large but can be made even larger with a different label.

**(E)** concludes that something is *impossible*, which is far stronger than the original argument—which says "very little" can be learned about successful spies who "normally only" reveal their methods when they are caught. Furthermore, **(E)** fails to include two groups of people, one of which provides more limited information than the other. Successful spies *could* reveal information, but in **(E)** there is no way to find out what would have happened had there been no intervention in the conflict.

### 24. (E) Principle (Identify/Assumption)

**Step 1: Identify the Question Type**

The question directly asks for a principle, which makes this an Identify the Principle question. Furthermore, it is said that the argument "requires assuming" the principle. This means that this would also work like a Necessary Assumption question, only with an answer that is in broader terms than usual.

**Step 2: Untangle the Stimulus**

The author argues that parents should be allowed to vote on behalf of their children, *thus* giving families fair representation. As evidence, the author points out that families are often overlooked in politics because families have underage children who cannot vote.

**Step 3: Make a Prediction**

Allowing parents to vote on behalf of their children would certainly allow families to get more representation in elections. After all, they would be allowed to cast votes for family members who couldn't previously vote. However, is this really *fair*? The author must assume so, which means the necessary principle here is that *more* representation is *fair* representation.

**Step 4: Evaluate the Answer Choices**

**(E)** is the assumed principle, connecting the increased number of votes to the idea of fairness.

**(A)** is a Faulty Use of Detail. The author does bemoan the lack of attention given to families, but the conclusion (and thus the argument) is ultimately about fair representation, not how much attention people get.

**(B)** is Out of Scope. The author's conclusion does not rest on the condition that children lack maturity. The only reason given for children not voting is that they are *underage*. Maturity has no bearing on the argument.

**(C)** is Extreme. The author only recommends giving parents the right to vote on behalf of their children. There's no mention of having to serve their children's interests. Perhaps the author believes votes cast on behalf of the children should represent the children's best interests, but the votes made by the adults (for the adults) may not have to. Either way, this is not necessary to the argument.

**(D)** is an Irrelevant Comparison. The author is not comparing people who *can* vote to people who *cannot*. Besides, the author is only arguing a certain action is fair, not judging any action as *not* fair.

### 25. (C) Weaken

**Step 1: Identify the Question Type**

The question directly asks for something that weakens the given argument.

**Step 2: Untangle the Stimulus**

The critic concludes that a newspaper's plan to avoid errors is not working. As evidence, the critic cites that the newspaper acknowledges more errors by printing corrections than a competing newspaper.

**Step 3: Make a Prediction**

The critic assumes that the greater number of corrections somehow indicates a failure to avoid errors. This overlooks the possibility that the newspaper *is* doing a better job at avoiding errors—it just also does a better job at admitting when it *does* make an error. Showing such an overlooked possibility would certainly weaken the critic's argument.

**Step 4: Evaluate the Answer Choices**

**(C)** weakens the argument. This suggests that the newspaper is just more diligent about acknowledging errors. Its competitor might make a *lot* more errors, but it might just not care enough to correct them.

**(A)** is an Irrelevant Comparison. No connection can be logically drawn between salary and avoiding errors.

**(B)** is an Irrelevant Comparison. How long the newspaper has been in business has no bearing on its ability to avoid errors.

**(D)** is a 180 at worst. If the newspaper uses more editors and *still* has to print more corrections, the critic's claim that the paper's plan isn't working is only helped.

**(E)** is Out of Scope. The size of the reporting staff has no bearing on whether the editorial staff is doing its job or not.

# Section II: Logic Games
## Game 1: Special Project Workers

| Q# | Question Type | Correct | Difficulty |
|---|---|---|---|
| 1 | Acceptability | C | ★ |
| 2 | "If" / Must Be True | D | ★ |
| 3 | Supply the If | A | ★★ |
| 4 | "If" / Must Be True | E | ★★ |
| 5 | Completely Determine | B | ★★★ |

## Game 2: 1920s History Archives Project

| Q# | Question Type | Correct | Difficulty |
|---|---|---|---|
| 6 | Acceptability | C | ★ |
| 7 | Supply the If | E | ★★ |
| 8 | "If" / Could Be True | A | ★ |
| 9 | How Many | D | ★★★ |
| 10 | "If" / Could Be True | E | ★★ |
| 11 | Must Be False (CANNOT Be True) | A | ★★ |

## Game 3: Antique Dealer Auction

| Q# | Question Type | Correct | Difficulty |
|---|---|---|---|
| 12 | Acceptability | C | ★ |
| 13 | Could Be True | B | ★★ |
| 14 | "If" / Could Be True | D | ★★ |
| 15 | Must Be False (CANNOT Be True) | A | ★★ |
| 16 | Could Be True | E | ★★★ |
| 17 | Could Be True | B | ★★★ |

## Game 4: Chorus Auditions

| Q# | Question Type | Correct | Difficulty |
|---|---|---|---|
| 18 | Acceptability | D | ★ |
| 19 | Must Be False (CANNOT Be True) | C | ★ |
| 20 | Could Be True | C | ★ |
| 21 | "If" / Could Be True | E | ★★ |
| 22 | Could Be True | B | ★★ |
| 23 | Rule Substitution | A | ★★★★ |

# Game 1: Special Project Workers

## Step 1: Overview

**Situation:** Workers being considered for a special project

**Entities:** Seven workers (Quinn, Ruiz, Smith, Taylor, Verma, Wells, Xue)

**Action:** Selection. Determine which workers will be selected for the special project.

**Limitations:** Exactly three workers will be selected. Furthermore, exactly one of those workers will be selected as project leader, adding a second level of selection.

## Step 2: Sketch

List the entities by initial. Because it is known how many people will be selected, an In/Out sketch can be used with three "In" slots and four "Out" slots. Be sure to label one "In" slot as the project leader.

```
          QRSTVWX
        In        Out
      __  __  __ | __  __
      p.l.       | __  __
```

## Step 3: Rules

**Rule 1** provides some Formal Logic. If Quinn or Ruiz is selected, that person must be project leader. This does *not* mean Quinn or Ruiz will definitely be selected, but either one must be project leader *if* selected.

$$Q \text{ or } R \longrightarrow \text{ project leader}$$

As an early deduction, it should be noted that this means Q and R cannot *both* be selected. Otherwise, they would both be project leaders, and there can only be one.

$$\begin{array}{c} \text{Never} \\ QR \end{array}$$

**Rule 2** is more Formal Logic. If Smith is selected, then so is Taylor. Draw that out and its contrapositive:

$$S \longrightarrow T$$
$$\sim T \longrightarrow \sim S$$

**Rule 3** is even more Formal Logic. If Wells is selected, then Ruiz and Verma are not. You can draw out this rule and its contrapositive:

$$W \longrightarrow \sim R \ \& \ \sim V$$
$$R \text{ or } V \longrightarrow \sim W$$

However, this rule can be interpreted more simply: it is impossible to select both Wells and Ruiz (because selecting one requires rejecting the other), and it is similarly impossible to select Wells and Verma.

$$\begin{array}{c} \text{Never} \\ WR \\ WV \end{array}$$

## Step 4: Deductions

Because every rule is conditional, it's difficult to make any substantial deductions until some condition is met. There is no specific worker who must or cannot be selected. And any worker could still be project leader. There's even one worker, Xue, who is completely unrestricted (i.e., a Floater)—which you can note with an asterisk in your entity list. There are no Blocks of Entities, no clear Limited Options, and no Established Entities. The only part of BLEND that can yield a meaningful deduction is the Numbers. Although there are too many outcomes to consider for who *is* selected, there are few deductions that can be made about who is *not* selected. First, because Quinn and Ruiz are both only able to be the project leader (Rule 1), at least one of them must not be selected. That means one of them will occupy one of the four "Out" slots. Furthermore, because Wells and Verma are mutually exclusive (Rule 3), one of the two of them also must *not* be selected.

```
          QRSTVWX*
        In        Out
      __  __  __ | Q/R  V/W
                 | __  __
```

Ruiz is a Duplication in the rules (in fact the only one), but the mutual exclusivity of Wells and Ruiz cannot also be built into the Master Sketch, because it's possible one or each is already represented by the "Q/R" and "V/W" in the first two "Out" slots. So, the Ruiz Duplication does not allow the rules to be logically combined in any meaningful way at this point. With so few deductions, it's important to be confident with the rules and consider each one when new conditions are presented.

## Step 5: Questions

### 1. (C) Acceptability

As with any Acceptability question, use the rules one at a time to eliminate answers that violate those rules.

**(B)** violates Rule 1 by having Quinn selected, but not as the leader. **(D)** violates Rule 2 by selecting Smith without Taylor. **(A)** violates Rule 3 by selecting Wells but also selecting Ruiz. **(E)** also violates Rule 3 by selecting Wells but also selecting Verma. That leaves **(C)** as the correct answer.

### 2. (D) "If" / Must Be True

For this question, Taylor and Wells are selected, and Taylor is the project leader. Because Taylor is the project leader, neither Quinn nor Ruiz can be project leader, so they cannot be selected at all (Rule 1). Because Wells is selected, Verma cannot be selected (Rule 3). That leaves Smith and Xue, either of whom could fill in the third spot on the project.

| In | | | Out | |
|----|----|----|----|----|
| T | W | S/X | Q | R |
| pl | | | V | X/S |

That makes **(D)** the correct answer.

### 3. (A) Supply the If

The correct answer will be a condition that would allow Verma to be project leader. The remaining answers would make it impossible for Verma to be project leader.

In order for Verma to be project leader, Quinn and Ruiz would have to be rejected. Otherwise, one of them would be project leader (Rule 1). Also, Wells would have to be rejected, otherwise Verma couldn't be selected for the project at all (Rule 3).

| In | | | Out | |
|---|---|---|---|---|
| V | _ | _ | Q | R |
| pl | | | W | |

That would leave Smith, Taylor, and Xue—two of whom must be selected and one of whom must be rejected. Getting rid of Taylor would also get rid of Smith (Rule 2). That wouldn't leave enough people on the project to work with Verma. Therefore, Taylor would *have* to be selected, which eliminates **(B)**, **(C)**, and **(E)**. And the project couldn't exclude Smith and Xue because, again, that wouldn't leave enough people on the project to work with Verma. That eliminates **(D)**, leaving **(A)** as the correct answer. Sure enough, if Quinn and Smith were rejected, Verma could be project leader on a team with Taylor and Xue.

| In | | | Out | |
|---|---|---|---|---|
| V | T | X | Q | R |
| pl | | | W | S |

### 4. (E) "If" / Must Be True

For this question, Taylor is not selected. In that case, Smith is also not selected (Rule 2). That leaves Quinn, Ruiz, Verma, Wells, and Xue. As noted in Step 4, Quinn and Ruiz cannot both be selected, or else there would be two project leaders (Rule 1). Also, Verma and Wells cannot both be selected (Rule 3). This creates some major Numbers restrictions. Between Quinn and Ruiz, only one can be selected. Same with Verma and Wells. That would account for two members. The third and final member would have to be the only remaining worker: Xue.

| In | | | Out | |
|---|---|---|---|---|
| R/Q | V/W | X | T | S |
| pl | | | Q/R | W/V |

That makes **(E)** the correct answer.

### 5. (B) Completely Determine

The correct answer to this question will create enough restrictions such that only one outcome is possible. The other four answers will still allow for multiple outcomes.

If neither Quinn nor Smith is selected, that would leave Ruiz, Taylor, Verma, Wells, and Xue. In that case, Wells could be selected along with Taylor and Xue. Or Wells could be left out, and any of the remaining three could be selected.

| In | | | Out | |
|---|---|---|---|---|
| _ | _ | _ | Q | S |
| | | | W/V | _ |

This leaves too many possibilities, so **(A)** can be eliminated.

If neither Quinn nor Taylor is selected, then Smith cannot be selected (Rule 2). That leaves Ruiz, Verma, Wells, and Xue. Wells cannot be selected, otherwise Ruiz and Verma would be rejected (Rule 3), leaving only two people for the project. With Wells out, that leaves three people: Ruiz, Verma, and Xue. Ruiz would be project leader (Rule 1).

| In | | | Out | |
|---|---|---|---|---|
| R | V | X | Q | T |
| pl | | | S | W |

That is the only possible outcome, making **(B)** the correct answer. For the record:

If neither Quinn nor Xue is selected, there are still plenty of outcomes. Wells could be selected with Smith and Taylor. Or Wells could be rejected, and either Ruiz or Verma could be selected with Smith and Taylor, among other outcomes.

| In | | | Out | |
|---|---|---|---|---|
| _ | _ | _ | Q | X |
| | | | W/V | _ |

There are too many possibilities, so that eliminates **(C)**.

If neither Ruiz nor Wells is selected, that leaves Quinn, Smith, Taylor, Verma, and Xue. Virtually any trio could be selected from that group, as long as Smith is not selected without Taylor.

| In | | | Out | |
|---|---|---|---|---|
| _ | _ | _ | R | W |
| | | | _ | _ |

This results in too many outcomes, so that eliminates **(D)**.

If neither Ruiz nor Verma is selected, that leaves Quinn, Smith, Taylor, Wells, and Xue. Again, as long as Smith is not selected without Taylor, any other trio is acceptable.

| In | | | Out | |
|---|---|---|---|---|
| _ | _ | _ | R | V |
| | | | _ | _ |

This leaves too many outcomes, so that eliminates **(E)**.

# Game 2: 1920s History Archives Project

## Step 1: Overview

**Situation:** Students being assigned to search archives for a history project

**Entities:** Six students (Louis, Mollie, Onyx, Ryan, Tiffany, Yoshio) and four archive years (1921, 1922, 1923, 1924)

**Action:** Sequencing/Selection Hybrid. Determine which students will be selected for the project (Selection), and place them in order of the years they must search (Sequencing).

**Limitations:** For the Selection element, exactly four of the six students will be chosen. For the Sequencing element, each individual year will be searched by exactly one student. That makes it standard 1:1 Sequencing.

## Step 2: Sketch

For the Sequencing element, a set of four numbered slots will suffice. You can write out the full year or just use the last digit of each year (1, 2, 3, 4). For the Selection element, simply list the students by initial and note that four out of the six will be selected. As the game proceeds, circle students that are chosen and cross out those who aren't.

LMORTY

Pick 4

___  ___  ___  ___
 1    2    3    4

## Step 3: Rules

**Rule 1** assigns Louis or Tiffany in 1923. That means at least one of them will be selected. However, it could be either one, and it is still possible that both are selected. In that case, one would be assigned to 1923, and the other could be assigned to any other year. For this rule, simply establish "L/T" in the slot for 1923.

**Rule 2** restricts Mollie. If she is selected, she can only be assigned to 1921 or 1922. This does not mean Mollie *must* be selected. However, it does mean that she cannot be assigned any other year. Since Louis or Tiffany is already established in 1923, simply add "~ M" under the slot for 1924.

**Rule 3** provides some Formal Logic for the selection. If Tiffany is selected, then so is Ryan. By contrapositive, if Ryan is not selected, then Tiffany is not.

T → R

~R → ~T

**Rule 4** provides more Formal Logic. If Ryan is selected, then Onyx must also be selected and assigned the year immediately before Ryan. By contrapositive, if Onyx is not selected, then neither is Ryan.

R → <u>O</u> <u>R</u>

~O → ~R

## Step 4: Deductions

The last rule is very significant. If Ryan is selected, that creates a block of Onyx immediately before Ryan. With Louis or Tiffany established in 1923, there is only way to assign the block of Onyx and Ryan: Onyx in 1921 and Ryan in 1922.

However, that only happens if Ryan *is* selected. If Ryan is *not* selected, that leads to even *more* deductions from Rule 3. At this point, there are major ramifications depending on whether Ryan is selected or not. That means Limited Options would be highly valuable.

In the first option, Ryan is selected. That means Onyx is selected and assigned immediately before Ryan. That could only happen by assigning Onyx to 1921 and Ryan to 1922. Louis or Tiffany will be assigned to 1923. That leaves 1924. Mollie cannot be assigned to 1924 (Rule 2), so Mollie can be crossed off. That leaves Yoshio for 1924, or either Louis or Tiffany—whoever is not assigned—to 1923.

I)        L M̸ Ⓞ Ⓡ T Y

 <u>O</u>  <u>R</u>  <u>L/T</u>  ___
 1    2     3      4

In the second option, Ryan is not selected. By Rule 3, Tiffany will also be left out. That means the remaining four students must be selected: Louis, Mollie, Onyx, and Yoshio. With Tiffany unavailable, that means Louis must be assigned to 1923. The only other restriction is that Mollie can only be assigned to 1921 or 1922. So, either Onyx or Yoshio must be assigned to 1924.

II)       Ⓛ Ⓜ Ⓞ R̸ T̸ Ⓨ

 ___  ___  <u>L</u>  <u>O/Y</u>
  1    2    3     4

## Step 5: Questions

### 6. (C) Acceptability

As with any Acceptability question, go through the rules one at a time, eliminating answers that violate those rules. Keep in mind that the answers are listed in chronological order: 1921, 1922, 1923, 1924.

**(A)** violates Rule 1 by assigning Ryan, and not Louis or Tiffany, to 1923. **(E)** violates Rule 2 by assigning Mollie to 1924. **(B)** violates Rule 3 by assigning Tiffany to the project without Ryan. **(D)** violates Rule 4 by assigning Ryan to the project without Onyx *immediately* before. That leaves **(C)** as the correct answer.

### 7. (E) Supply the If

The correct answer will be a condition that forces Mollie to be assigned to 1922. The wrong answers will all allow Mollie to be assigned to another year or even go unassigned.

Mollie can only be assigned to 1921 or 1922, so the correct answer is likely to establish another student to 1921. If Onyx is assigned to 1921, then 1922 would be the only year left for Mollie. However, it's also possible that Mollie is not assigned at all (as seen in Option I). That eliminates **(B)**.

If Yoshio is assigned to 1921, Louis or Tiffany is assigned to 1923. In that case, there is no longer space for Onyx and Ryan to be consecutive. That means Ryan cannot be assigned at all (Rule 4), which also means Tiffany is not assigned (Rule 3). That means everyone else must be assigned, including Mollie. (Option II makes this clear, as Yoshio could only be assigned to 1921 in Option II.) With Yoshio in 1921, Mollie would have to be assigned to 1922. That's what the question is looking for, making **(E)** the correct answer. For the record:

If Louis is assigned to 1924, Tiffany would be assigned to 1923 (Rule 1). With Tiffany assigned to 1923, Ryan would have to be assigned (Rule 3) with Onyx immediately before (Rule 4). They would be assigned to 1921 and 1922, as seen in Option I. Mollie couldn't be assigned at all, so that eliminates **(A)** and **(D)**.

If Onyx is assigned to 1924 (as could happen in Option II), Mollie could still be assigned to 1921 *or* 1922. That eliminates **(C)**.

## 8. (A) "If" / Could Be True

For this question, Ryan and Yoshio are both assigned—which only happens in Option I. With Ryan assigned, Onyx is also assigned and immediately before Ryan (Rule 4). With Tiffany or Louis assigned to 1923, Onyx and Ryan can only be assigned to 1921 and 1922, respectively. That leaves 1924 for Yoshio.

$$\frac{O}{1} \quad \frac{R}{2} \quad \frac{L/T}{3} \quad \frac{Y}{4}$$

With that, only **(A)** is possible and is thus the correct answer.

## 9. (D) How Many

The question asks for the number of students who could be assigned to 1921. Limited Options help a lot with this question. In Option I, only Onyx could be assigned to 1921. In Option II, Louis is assigned to 1923. Any of the remaining three students that are selected—Mollie, Onyx, or Yoshio—could be assigned to 1921. So, Mollie, Onyx, and Yoshio are the only three students who could be assigned to 1921, making **(D)** the correct answer.

As further proof, Ryan cannot be assigned to 1921 because that would leave no previous year for Onyx, violating Rule 4. Also, neither Louis nor Tiffany could be assigned to 1921. If that happened, one would be assigned to 1921 and the other to 1923. Tiffany would definitely be assigned, but that would force Ryan to be assigned (Rule 3), which would force a block with Onyx (Rule 4) that would be impossible to place. So,

Ryan, Louis, and Tiffany could *not* be assigned to 1921. That leaves the other three: Mollie, Onyx, and Yoshio.

## 10. (E) "If" / Could Be True

For this question, Yoshio is not assigned at all. That leaves five students. Ryan would have to be assigned, otherwise Ryan would be out, eliminating Tiffany (Rule 3) and leaving only three students.

With Ryan selected, Onyx has to be selected and assigned the year before. With Louis or Tiffany assigned to 1923, Onyx and Ryan would have to be assigned to 1921 and 1922, respectively (as seen in Option I). That leaves 1924 open. Mollie cannot be assigned to 1924 (Rule 2), so she is not assigned at all. With Mollie and Yoshio both out, that means Louis and Tiffany are both assigned. One will be assigned to 1923, the other will be assigned to 1924.

L̶ M̶ (O)(R)(T) Y̶

$$\frac{O}{1} \quad \frac{R}{2} \quad \frac{L/T}{3} \quad \frac{T/L}{4}$$

So, Louis, Ryan, and Tiffany *are* assigned for sure, and Onyx is assigned to 1921. That leaves **(E)** as the only remaining answer. Louis *could* be assigned to 1924, so **(E)** is correct.

## 11. (A) Must Be False (CANNOT Be True)

The correct answer will be a student who cannot be assigned to 1922. The remaining students all *could* be.

Limited Options help a lot here. In Option I, Ryan is assigned to 1922. That eliminates **(D)**. In Option II, with Louis assigned to 1923, Mollie, Onyx, or Yoshio could be assigned to 1922. That eliminates **(B)**, **(C)**, and **(E)**, leaving **(A)** as the correct answer.

For further proof, if Louis were assigned to 1922, then Tiffany would be assigned to 1923 (Rule 1). With Tiffany assigned, Ryan would have to be assigned (Rule 3), with Onyx assigned the previous year (Rule 4). With 1922 and 1923 filled, the Onyx and Ryan block could not be placed. This is impossible, so Louis cannot be assigned to 1922.

$$\frac{}{1} \quad \frac{L}{2} \quad \frac{T}{3} \quad \frac{}{4}$$
$$\boxed{O \quad R}$$

# Game 3: Antique Dealer Auction

## Step 1: Overview

**Situation:** An antique dealer auctioning off antiques at a shop's grand opening

**Entities:** Six antiques (harmonica, lamp, mirror, sundial, table, vase)

**Action:** Loose Sequencing. Determine the order in which the antiques are auctioned, from June 1 to June 6. The only indication that this is Loose Sequencing is the rules, which all establish relative ordering with no defined spacing. The first rule is admittedly strict, but the ultimate sketch and treatment of the entities work much more like a Loose Sequencing game than a Strict one.

**Limitations:** The dealer will auction each antique, exactly one per day. There are no ties in the sequence.

## Step 2: Sketch

As with any Sequencing game, list the entities by initial. Because this is Loose Sequencing, no sketch is needed up front. It would be understandable to want a series of numbered slots, but they would likely go unused for the rest of the game.

## Step 3: Rules

**Rule 1** prevents the sundial from being auctioned first. If you've drawn slots, "~ S" could be added under the first slot. Otherwise, draw a note to the side: "S ≠ 1."

**Rule 2** provides Formal Logic. If the harmonica is auctioned earlier than the lamp, then so is the mirror. By contrapositive, if the mirror is *not* auctioned earlier than the lamp (i.e., the mirror *is* auctioned later), then the harmonica is not auctioned earlier (i.e., is later) than the lamp.

$$H-L \rightarrow M-L$$
$$L-M \rightarrow L-H$$

This rule allows for three possibilities:

$$\begin{array}{c} H \diagdown \\ \phantom{}\diagup L \quad or \\ M \end{array}$$

$$\begin{array}{c} \diagup M \\ L \quad or \\ \diagdown H \end{array}$$

$$M-L-H$$

**Rule 3** dictates that the sundial be auctioned before the mirror and the vase, but does not indicate whether the mirror should be auctioned before the vase or vice versa.

$$\begin{array}{c} \diagup M \\ S \\ \diagdown V \end{array}$$

**Rule 4** requires the table to be auctioned earlier than the harmonica or the vase, *but not both*. So, if the table is auctioned earlier than the harmonica, the table must be auctioned *later* than the vase. Similarly, if the table is

auctioned earlier than the vase, then it must be auctioned later than the harmonica. In short, the table will be auctioned before one and after the other:

$$V-T-H$$
$$or$$
$$H-T-V$$

## Step 4: Deductions

Rule 4 presents two possible orders for half of the antiques (whereas Rule 2 allows for three possible orders). Further, each order includes the vase, which is also mentioned in Rule 3 along with two other antiques. That means each option would create connections among five of the six antiques. That warrants setting up Limited Options based on Rule 4.

In the first option, the table will be auctioned before the harmonica, which means the table will be auctioned after the vase. The vase will be auctioned later than the sundial (Rule 3). The sundial is also auctioned before the mirror, but that is not connected to any of the other antiques so far.

$$I) \quad \begin{array}{c} \diagup M \\ S \\ \diagdown V-T-H \end{array}$$

In that case, the sundial is auctioned before every other listed antique. However, by Rule 1, it cannot be auctioned first. That leaves one antique, the lamp, to be first. With the lamp first, the sundial will be auctioned second. The remaining antiques will be the vase, table, and harmonica, in that order, with the mirror being auctioned at any point in between.

$$I) \quad \begin{array}{c} \diagup M \\ L-S \\ \diagdown V-T-H \end{array}$$

In the second option, the table will be auctioned before the vase, which means the table will be auctioned after the harmonica. The sundial will also be auctioned before the vase (Rule 3), but there is no connection between the sundial and the table. Further, the sundial will be auctioned before the mirror, which is not connected to anything else. That leaves the lamp, which is only limited by Rule 2. However, Rule 2 is conditional, so the lamp cannot be placed with certainty.

$$II) \quad \begin{array}{c} \diagup M \\ S \quad L? \\ H-T-V \end{array}$$

## Step 5: Questions

### 12. (C) Acceptability

As with any Acceptability question, use the rules one at a time to eliminate answers until there is one answer left that does not violate any rule.

**(D)** violates Rule 1 by placing the sundial first. **(A)** violates Rule 2 by having the harmonica before the lamp, but then having the mirror *after* the lamp. **(E)** violates Rule 3 by having the sundial before the mirror but not the vase. **(B)** violates

Rule 4 by having the table at the end, earlier than neither the harmonica nor the vase. That leaves **(C)** as the correct answer.

### 13. (B) Could Be True

The correct answer will be the only one that is possible. The other four must be false.

The table has to be auctioned between the harmonica and the vase (Rule 4). If the table is auctioned on the 2nd, the harmonica would have to be auctioned on the 1st because the vase still needs to be auctioned after the sundial (Rule 3). With the harmonica on the 1st, it will certainly be auctioned earlier than the lamp. That means the mirror must also be auctioned earlier than the lamp (Rule 2). But then the lamp could not be auctioned on the 3rd because there would be no room for the mirror before it.

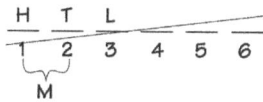

$$\begin{array}{cccccc} H & T & L & & & \\ \hline 1 & 2 & 3 & 4 & 5 & 6 \\ \end{array}$$
$$\underbrace{\phantom{1\ 2}}_{M}$$

**(A)** is thus impossible and can be eliminated.

The sundial could be auctioned on the 2nd, and it must precede the vase, which could certainly be on the 3rd. Then the lamp could be on the 1st, with the remaining antiques taking up the remaining spots.

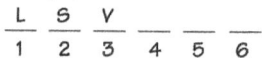

$$\begin{array}{cccccc} L & S & V & & & \\ \hline 1 & 2 & 3 & 4 & 5 & 6 \\ \end{array}$$

This is all seen as possible in Option I. That makes **(B)** the correct answer. For the record:

The sundial must be auctioned before the mirror and the vase (Rule 3), so that eliminates **(C)** and **(D)**. Likewise, if the sundial was auctioned on the 4th and the table on the 5th, that would leave no room for both the mirror and the vase, which both have to be after the sundial (Rule 3).

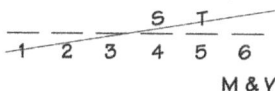

$$\begin{array}{cccccc} & & & S & T & \\ \hline 1 & 2 & 3 & 4 & 5 & 6 \\ \end{array}$$
$$\phantom{11111111111}M\ \&\ V$$

That eliminates **(E)**.

### 14. (D) "If" / Could Be True

For this question, the table will be auctioned later than the mirror and the vase (which can only happen in Option I). If the table is auctioned later than the vase, then it must be auctioned earlier than the harmonica (Rule 4). The mirror and the vase, in either order, must both be auctioned after the sundial (Rule 3). At that point, everything would be auctioned after the sundial, but the sundial cannot be auctioned first (Rule 1). That means the remaining antique, the lamp, would be first. The sundial would be second. The table and harmonica would be fifth and sixth, respectively. The only thing that cannot be determined is the order of the vase and the mirror.

$$L - S \overset{\displaystyle \overset{M}{\diagup}}{\underset{\displaystyle V}{\diagdown}} T - H$$

With that, only **(D)** is possible and is thus the correct answer.

### 15. (A) Must Be False (CANNOT Be True)

The correct answer for this question will be the antique that cannot be auctioned immediately before the vase. The remaining four antiques *could* be auctioned immediately before the vase.

By Rule 4, if the table is auctioned earlier than the vase, then the harmonica would be auctioned earlier than the table. And if the table is auctioned earlier than the harmonica, then the vase would be auctioned earlier than the table.

$$V - T - H$$
$$\text{or}$$
$$H - T - V$$

That means the table must be auctioned in between the harmonica and the vase. Therefore, the harmonica could never be immediately before the vase, making **(A)** the correct answer.

### 16. (E) Could Be True

The correct answer will be the only one that is possible. The remaining four answers all must be false.

The mirror must be auctioned after the sundial. If the mirror was auctioned on the 2nd, the sundial would be auctioned on the 1st, violating Rule 1. That eliminates **(A)**.

If the lamp is auctioned on the 2nd, the harmonica could not be auctioned on the 1st because that would require the mirror to be auctioned before the lamp (Rule 2), and there would be no room for that to happen. The sundial could not be on the 1st (Rule 1), nor could the mirror or vase (Rule 3). And the table has to be auctioned between the harmonica and the vase (Rule 4), so the table couldn't be on the 1st. That would leave nothing to be on the 1st.

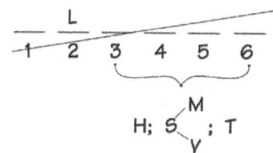

$$\begin{array}{cccccc} & L & & & & \\ \hline 1 & 2 & 3 & 4 & 5 & 6 \\ \end{array}$$
$$\phantom{11111}H;\ S \overset{\diagup}{\underset{V}{\diagdown}} ;\ T$$

That's not possible, which eliminates **(B)**.

The vase must be auctioned after the sundial. If the vase was auctioned on the 2nd, the sundial would be auctioned on the 1st, violating Rule 1. That eliminates **(C)**.

If the lamp is auctioned on the 3rd, the sundial could not be auctioned on the 1st (Rule 1), nor could the mirror or the vase (Rule 3) or the table (Rule 4). That leaves the harmonica. If the harmonica were on the 1st, the mirror would have to be before the lamp (Rule 2), so the mirror would be on the 2nd. But that would not leave room for the sundial before the mirror, violating Rule 3.

```
        S
        \
   H    M    L
  ──   ──   ──   ──   ──   ──
  1    2    3    4    5    6
```

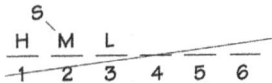

This is impossible, which eliminates **(D)**.

That leaves **(E)** as the correct answer, which is possible in either of the two options. Here is an example of each:

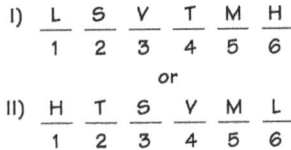

```
I)   L    S    V    T    M    H
    ──   ──   ──   ──   ──   ──
    1    2    3    4    5    6
              or
II)  H    T    S    V    M    L
    ──   ──   ──   ──   ──   ──
    1    2    3    4    5    6
```

## 17. (B) Could Be True

The correct answer here could be true, which means the remaining answers all must be false.

The sundial cannot be auctioned on the 5th because there would be no room for both the vase and the mirror afterward, violating Rule 3. That eliminates **(A)**.

The sundial could be auctioned on the 4th, though. Then the mirror and vase would be on the 5th and 6th, in either order. The remaining antiques would be the harmonica, table, and vase, in that order or the reverse (by Rule 4).

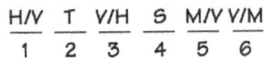

```
  H/V   T   V/H   S   M/V  V/M
  ──   ──   ──   ──   ──   ──
  1    2    3    4    5    6
```

This is possible, making **(B)** the correct answer. For the record:

If the lamp were on the 5th and the mirror were on the 6th, the contrapositive of Rule 2 would be triggered, which would require the lamp to also precede the harmonica. However, with the 5th and 6th slots filled, there is no more room after the lamp, so this is impossible. That eliminates **(C)**.

If the table were on the 3rd and the lamp on the 4th, the sundial could not be on the 1st (Rule 1), nor could the mirror or vase (Rule 3). That would leave the harmonica on the 1st. By Rule 2, the mirror would have to be before the lamp, thus on the 2nd. But that would violate Rule 3 because there would be no room for the sundial before the mirror.

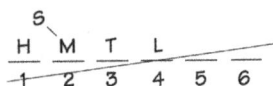

```
        S
        \
   H    M    T    L
  ──   ──   ──   ──   ──   ──
  1    2    3    4    5    6
```

That eliminates **(D)**.

The table has to be auctioned between the harmonica and the vase (Rule 4), so the harmonica and vase cannot be consecutive. That eliminates **(E)**.

# Game 4: Chorus Auditions

### Step 1: Overview

**Situation:** Singers auditioning for a chorus director

**Entities:** Six singers (Kammer, Lugo, Trillo, Waite, Yoshida, Zinn)

**Action:** Strict Sequencing. Determine the order in which the singers audition. Even though each singer's audition is recorded or not recorded, there is no Matching component, because it's already announced which singers are recorded and which aren't. If that information were not already concrete, then this would be a Sequencing/Matching Hybrid.

**Limitations:** The six singers will all be auditioned, and auditions take place one after the other, so this is standard 1:1 Sequencing. It's also noted that two of the singers, Kammer and Lugo, will be recorded while the others will not.

### Step 2: Sketch

List the singers by initial, and set up a series of six numbered slots. Be sure to distinguish the two singers that are recorded; there are many ways to do so. You can just label the entity list with those that are recorded and those that aren't, you can put the recorded ones in uppercase and the non-recorded ones in lowercase, you can put an "r" under each recorded singer and an "n" under each non-recorded one, etc. It doesn't matter which you choose, just make sure they're at least distinguished in the entity list.

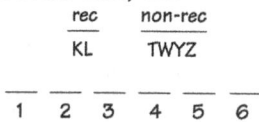

| rec | non-rec |
|-----|---------|
| KL  | TWYZ    |

___  ___  ___  ___  ___  ___
 1    2    3    4    5    6

### Step 3: Rules

**Rule 1** establishes the fourth audition as non-recorded. Depending on your notation, you may consider adding "n" under the fourth slot. You may alternatively or additionally want to put "~ K" and "~ L" underneath the slot, which would also capture the rule.

**Rule 2** establishes the fifth audition as recorded. Depending on your notation, you may consider adding "r" under the fifth slot. You may alternatively or additionally want to put "K/L" in the slot itself, which would also capture the rule.

**Rule 3** requires Waite to audition before both recorded singers (Kammer and Lugo). Kammer and Lugo could still audition in either order. There's no need to necessarily indicate recorded/non-recorded because the sequence already completely represents the rule.

```
        K
      W
        L
```

**Rule 4** requires Kammer to audition before Trillo. That can be immediately combined with Rule 3.

```
      K—T
    W
      L
```

**Rule 5** requires Zinn to audition before Yoshida.

```
    Z—Y
```

### Step 4: Deductions

Most of the deductions come from the orders established in the last three rules. That alone leads to a lot of restrictions about which entities *can't* be in certain slots (e.g., per Rule 4, Zinn can't be last and Yoshida can't be first). However, there's one more deduction to consider first. One of the recorded sessions (Kammer or Lugo) will be fifth (Rule 2). The other recorded session cannot be fourth (Rule 1), nor can it be first because Waite must audition beforehand (Rule 3). That means the other recorded session must be second, third, or sixth. However, if it were sixth, that would mean the last two sessions would both be recorded. In that case, it would be impossible for Kammer to audition before Trillo (a non-recorded audition). Therefore, the other recorded session cannot be sixth, so it has to be either second or third. That allows for Limited Options.

If the other recorded session is second, then Waite would have to audition first. Kammer and Lugo would be second and fifth, in either order. Trillo, Yoshida, and Zinn would fill in the remaining spots. Because Zinn has to precede Yoshida (Rule 5), Zinn could not be last and Yoshida could not be third.

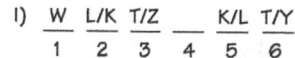

| I) | W | L/K | T/Z |   | K/L | T/Y |
|----|---|-----|-----|---|-----|-----|
|    | 1 | 2   | 3   | 4 | 5   | 6   |

If the other recorded session is third, Waite would audition first or second. Kammer and Lugo would be third and fifth, in either order. Trillo would have to audition after Kammer, so Trillo could not be first or second, and thus must be fourth or sixth.

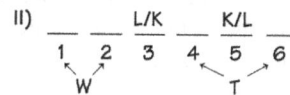

| II) | ___ | ___ | L/K | ___ | K/L | ___ |
|-----|-----|-----|-----|-----|-----|-----|
|     | 1   | 2   | 3   | 4   | 5   | 6   |

(W under 1/2, T under 4/6)

Yoshida has to audition after Zinn, so Yoshida also cannot be first or second—otherwise, it would be in the first two auditions with Waite, leaving no room for Zinn. That would leave Zinn as the only other singer who could audition first or second along with Waite, in either order. That means Trillo and Yoshida would be fourth or sixth, in either order.

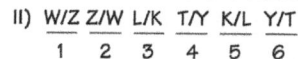

| II) | W/Z | Z/W | L/K | T/Y | K/L | Y/T |
|-----|-----|-----|-----|-----|-----|-----|
|     | 1   | 2   | 3   | 4   | 5   | 6   |

### Step 5: Questions

#### 18. (D) Acceptability

Use the rules one at a time to eliminate answers that violate the rules. The one answer that doesn't violate the rules is acceptable and thus correct. Be sure to refer to the entity list to remember who is recorded and who is not.

**(E)** violates Rule 1 by placing Lugo (a recorded singer) fourth. **(C)** violates Rule 2 by placing Zinn (a non-recorded singer) fifth. **(A)** violates Rule 3 by placing Waite after Kammer (a recorded singer). Neither of the remaining answers violates Rule 4. **(B)** violates Rule 5 by placing Yoshida before Zinn. That leaves **(D)** as the correct answer.

## 19. (C) Must Be False (CANNOT Be True)

The correct answer to this question will be someone who cannot be second. The remaining four answers list singers who *could*.

The second singer could be either recorded singer (Kammer or Lugo), as long as Waite auditions first (as seen in Option I). That eliminates **(A)** and **(B)**.

If Trillo auditioned second, Kammer would have to audition first (Rule 4). However, that would violate Rule 3 by leaving no space for Waite before Kammer. This is impossible, making **(C)** the correct answer. For the record:

If the third singer were a recorded singer (Kammer or Lugo), then the first and second singer would be Waite and Zinn, in either order (as seen in Option II). That means either of those singers could be second, which eliminates **(D)** and **(E)**.

## 20. (C) Could Be True

The correct answer will be a singer who could audition sixth. The other answers will list singers who absolutely cannot audition sixth.

By Rules 3, 4, and 5, Kammer, Waite, and Zinn all must audition earlier than at least one other singer. None of them could be sixth. That eliminates **(A)**, **(D)**, and **(E)**.

If Lugo auditioned sixth, then Kammer would audition fifth (Rule 2). That would leave no room for Trillo after Kammer, violating Rule 4. So, Lugo could not be sixth, eliminating **(B)**. That leaves **(C)** as the correct answer, which can be verified in the sketch for the next question of the set.

## 21. (E) "If" / Could Be True

For this question, Kammer will audition immediately before Yoshida. Kammer must also audition before Trillo (Rule 4) and after Waite (Rule 3). Yoshida must audition after Zinn (Rule 5).

```
        Z
         \
         KY—T
         /
        W
         \
          L
```

The fifth audition must be Kammer or Lugo, but Kammer must now audition before Yoshida and Trillo. That means Lugo auditions fifth. The rest of the order has already been determined: Waite and Zinn will audition (in either order)

before the block of Kammer and Yoshida, which must occur before Trillo auditions:

| W/Z | Z/W | K | Y | L | T |
|-----|-----|---|---|---|---|
| 1 | 2 | 3 | 4 | 5 | 6 |

With that, only **(E)** is possible, making that the correct answer.

## 22. (B) Could Be True

The correct answer will be a time Yoshida *could* audition. The others will list times Yoshida *could not* audition.

The quickest way to answer this question is to look at the sketch for the previous question. In that sketch, Yoshida auditioned fourth, making **(B)** the correct answer.

Limited Options also help. In both options, Yoshida is limited to the fourth and sixth auditions. Sixth is not an answer choice, so the correct answer is that Yoshida could be fourth.

## 23. (A) Rule Substitution

For this question, Rule 3 is removed from the game. The correct answer will be a rule that could replace Rule 3 without changing anything from the original setup. In other words, it will reestablish the original rule without adding any new restrictions.

The original rule required Waite to audition before both recorded auditions (Kammer and Lugo). By Rule 4, Kammer has to audition before Trillo, which means Waite would have been before Trillo, too. One recorded session is fifth. The other cannot be sixth without violating Rule 4, and it cannot be fourth without violating Rule 1. A recorded session also can't be first per Rule 3. So, the other recorded audition must be second or third. To restore Rule 3, the correct answer would have to force Waite before the other recorded audition (i.e., Waite must be first or second, and no recorded audition could be first) without adding any new restrictions.

If Zinn's is the only audition that could be earlier than Waite's, then Waite could only be first or second. That's a great start. If Waite goes first, it's automatically before everything. If Waite goes second, this rule makes Zinn first, so Waite would again audition before both recorded sessions. Further, neither of the remaining non-recorded auditions could have been first (not Trillo by Rule 4 nor Yoshida by Rule 6). Therefore, the original rule is restored without adding any new restrictions. That makes **(A)** the correct answer. For the record:

Requiring Waite to audition consecutively with Zinn does not force Waite to audition before a recorded session, and it adds a restriction that was not originally in place. (Waite and Zinn could be separated in Option I.) That eliminates **(B)**.

Requiring Waite to audition before Lugo forces Waite to audition before *one* of the recorded sessions, but still does not force Waite to audition before *both* recorded sessions (including Kammer's). That eliminates **(C)**.

Waite was always restricted to the first or second audition. However, adding that rule doesn't force Waite to audition before Kammer and Lugo. Kammer or Lugo could still audition first, which was not allowed by the initial rule. That eliminates **(D)**.

Adding **(E)** does restore the deduction that the first audition could never be recorded. However, adding just that restriction does not force Waite to audition before Kammer and Lugo. This places no restriction on Waite and would even allow Waite to go last.

$$\frac{Z \quad Y \quad K \quad T \quad L \quad \cancel{W}}{\cancel{1} \quad 2 \quad 3 \quad 4 \quad 5 \quad 6}$$

This does not restore the original rule, which eliminates **(E)**.

# Section III: Logical Reasoning

| Q# | Question Type | Correct | Difficulty |
|---|---|---|---|
| 1 | Flaw | A | ★ |
| 2 | Strengthen | D | ★ |
| 3 | Inference | B | ★ |
| 4 | Role of a Statement | C | ★ |
| 5 | Flaw | E | ★ |
| 6 | Principle (Identify/Strengthen) | B | ★ |
| 7 | Inference | E | ★ |
| 8 | Strengthen/Weaken (Evaluate the Argument) | A | ★ |
| 9 | Paradox | E | ★ |
| 10 | Assumption (Sufficient) | D | ★ |
| 11 | Principle (Identify/Inference) | E | ★★ |
| 12 | Assumption (Necessary) | B | ★ |
| 13 | Parallel Reasoning | A | ★★★ |
| 14 | Role of a Statement | C | ★ |
| 15 | Flaw | C | ★★ |
| 16 | Paradox | B | ★★ |
| 17 | Role of a Statement | A | ★★ |
| 18 | Main Point | C | ★★★★ |
| 19 | Role of a Statement | B | ★★★ |
| 20 | Assumption (Sufficient) | C | ★★★ |
| 21 | Strengthen | A | ★★★ |
| 22 | Inference (EXCEPT) | E | ★ |
| 23 | Strengthen/Weaken (Evaluate the Argument) | C | ★★★★ |
| 24 | Inference | E | ★★★★ |
| 25 | Parallel Flaw | D | ★★★★ |
| 26 | Weaken | D | ★ |

**KAPLAN**

## 1. (A) Flaw

### Step 1: Identify the Question Type

The question asks why the argument is "vulnerable to criticism," which means the correct answer will describe the argument's flaw.

### Step 2: Untangle the Stimulus

A nonprofit organization sent a fund-raising letter to 5,000 people and included a survey about a social issue. The author concludes that most of those people agree with the organization's position on that issue because 283 out of the 300 people who responded agree with the organization's position.

### Step 3: Make a Prediction

The author seems to ignore the fact that the survey accompanied a fund-raising letter. People who disagree with the organization are more likely to throw the survey out when they see the fund-raising letter. The people who respond are far more likely to be the people who side with the organization in the first place. And given how relatively few people responded (a mere 6%), the author makes the classic mistake of faulty representation: judging the opinions of a larger population based on a sample group that is likely to be biased.

### Step 4: Evaluate the Answer Choices

(A) describes the flaw: drawing a conclusion about a population (all 5,000 people) based on the opinions of a potentially unrepresentative subgroup (the 300 people who responded to the fund-raising letter).

(B) is Out of Scope. This was a one-time survey. No assumption is made about whether opinions would change "on different occasions."

(C) is Out of Scope. There's no reason to question the accuracy of the responses.

(D) gets the logic backward. The evidence is about a small group (the respondents), and the conclusion is about a larger population (all 5,000 people), not the other way around.

(E) is a 180. The author does not assume, but completely *overlooks*, this potential influence.

## 2. (D) Strengthen

### Step 1: Identify the Question Type

The question directly asks for something that strengthens the given argument.

### Step 2: Untangle the Stimulus

The author concludes that the Roman empire's fall was caused by an unstable climate. The evidence is that the Roman empire fell during a time of climate fluctuation, a condition that makes various aspects of life difficult.

### Step 3: Make a Prediction

This is a terrific example of correlation versus causation. The author assumes that two things coinciding (climate fluctuation and the fall of the Roman empire) indicate that one thing *caused* the other (climate fluctuation caused the fall). However, the correlation only involves one set of data: what the climate was like when the empire fell. What about when the empire was doing well? What was the climate like then? The author assumes it was stable, which the correct answer should validate.

### Step 4: Evaluate the Answer Choices

(D) helps the author out. If this were true, the correlation would be more consistent. Climate stable? Empire good. Climate unstable? Empire falls. That makes it more likely that the climate was responsible.

(A) is a 180. This suggests that political failures, and *not* the climate, were at fault.

(B) is a 180, suggesting that climate is not as much a factor as the author claims.

(C) is a 180, placing fault on poor farming practices rather than the climate.

(E) is an Irrelevant Comparison. It indicates that food production was higher around the time of the fall than at the start of the decline, but there's no information about what production was like prior to that time period. More importantly, it does nothing to confirm that the *climate* was responsible for any change in food production.

## 3. (B) Inference

### Step 1: Identify the Question Type

The question asks for something that would fill in the blank at the end of the argument. That blank is preceded by [*t*]*herefore*, which means the blank will be filled by something that logically follows the previous information. That makes this an Inference question.

### Step 2: Untangle the Stimulus

The manager states that naturally gifted salespeople are rare, but suggests that many salespeople can *appear* naturally gifted if they have a good manager.

### Step 3: Make a Prediction

The blank is preceded by *should*, which makes it a recommendation. If good managers can really turn a bunch of average salespeople into superstar performers, that would seem better than waiting around hoping to find that rare natural superstar. The correct answer will be a recommendation that favors using good managers.

### Step 4: Evaluate the Answer Choices

(B) is supported.

**(A)** is a Distortion. Training would be better than hoping to hire a natural superstar, but evaluation may still be equally important to make sure the training is working right. Furthermore, it's not clear that managers are responsible for training and evaluation, so **(A)** is not a logical conclusion.

**(C)** is not supported. There's nothing to suggest that reducing responsibility will make a manager any better.

**(D)** is not supported. If natural superstars are so rare, it would actually seem counterproductive to move them away from sales. And there's no indication that a gifted salesperson would be a good manager.

**(E)** is Out of Scope. The manager makes no mention of rewarding anyone, let alone favoring the naturally talented employees.

### 4. (C) Role of a Statement

#### Step 1: Identify the Question Type

The question presents a claim from the stimulus and asks for the role it plays in the argument, making this a Role of a Statement question. Start by finding the claim and underlining or putting a mark next to it. Then break the argument into evidence and conclusion, and determine how that claim fits in.

#### Step 2: Untangle the Stimulus

Economists have a rule: demand and price are inversely proportional. In other words, the lower the price, the higher the demand, and vice versa. The author provides an example: as steel prices dropped, more steel was purchased. *Nevertheless*, the author sees a problem. *Obviously*, the author concludes there are exceptions to the rule, as evidenced by lace. When lace prices dropped, so did demand.

#### Step 3: Make a Prediction

The author is not disputing the economists entirely, but is saying their rule has exceptions, i.e., it doesn't always work. So, how does the claim in question (regarding steel) fit in to this argument? Well, steel is an example in which the economist's rule *does* work (prices down, demand up). So, the role of that claim is to illustrate how the economist's rule *can* work, even if the author later argues it doesn't *always* apply.

#### Step 4: Evaluate the Answer Choices

**(C)** is a match. It illustrates the economist's generalization, which the author concludes does not always hold.

**(A)** is Out of Scope. The author merely presents the claim as an example. It is never "described as inadequate evidence" for anything.

**(B)** is a 180. The steel is consistent with the generalization. *Lace* was brought up as an exception.

**(D)** is a Distortion. It definitely fits the economists' view, but it is just an example. It was never said to "lead economists to embrace" that view.

**(E)** is a Distortion. The author never suggests modifying the assumption, just that there are exceptions. Also, steel is consistent with the economists' view. There is only one counterexample: lace.

### 5. (E) Flaw

#### Step 1: Identify the Question Type

The question directly asks for the flaw in the argument. Furthermore, it indicates that the flaw will be an overlooked possibility.

#### Step 2: Untangle the Stimulus

The resident concludes ([*h*]ence) that at least 60 percent of local homes have integrity problems because 30 percent have inadequate drainage and 30 percent have structural defects.

#### Step 3: Make a Prediction

The numbers certainly add up—as long as each group in the evidence is entirely independent. In other words, the author assumes that the houses with inadequate drainage and the ones with structural defects are two completely separate groups. If there is any overlap (i.e., houses with *both* problems), then the math doesn't hold up. The author overlooks the possibility of overlap.

#### Step 4: Evaluate the Answer Choices

**(E)** is correct.

**(A)** is a Distortion. The argument is about percentages. It doesn't matter if there are 10 houses or 10,000 houses.

**(B)** is a 180 and a Distortion. The author *assumes* inadequate drainage is a problem, so that isn't overlooked. And, even though the author may not say that all *problems* with integrity are *unsafe*, overlooking that possibility is not a flaw of the argument.

**(C)** is Out of Scope. The author is only concerned with the percentage of problems, not how easily fixed they are.

**(D)** is not overlooked. The author's argument is only about houses that *do* have problems. The author only claims that at least 60 percent have problems. The author could very well feel the other 40 percent are problem-free.

### 6. (B) Principle (Identify/Strengthen)

#### Step 1: Identify the Question Type

The question directly asks for a principle that will "justify the reasoning" given. That makes this an Identify the Principle question that acts like a Strengthen question.

### Step 2: Untangle the Stimulus

The author concludes ([s]o) that people shouldn't regret the missed opportunities of youth. As evidence, the author mentions how decisions impact our lives. The choices we made led to cherished relationships. If we had chosen differently and seized those opportunities, we may never have developed those relationships.

### Step 3: Make a Prediction

The author reaches a conclusion about what we shouldn't regret based on evidence of the cherished relationships we have. The assumption is that we shouldn't regret any decision that led us to those cherished relationships. The correct answer will express that idea, just in broader terms.

### Step 4: Evaluate the Answer Choices

**(B)** validates the author's assumption.

**(A)** is a Distortion. The author is only worried about the quality of the relationships, not whether a different decision would have gotten us *more*.

**(C)** is a 180. The author argues that we shouldn't regret the decisions that *did* have a big effect; they gave us the close relationships we cherish.

**(D)** is Out of Scope. The author is not concerned about how deeply we cherish the relationships we have. Also, the author claims we *shouldn't* regret our decisions. There's no information about people who *do* regret them.

**(E)** is Out of Scope. The author doesn't discuss the number of relationships one has, whether it be *few* or many. And this ignores the author's conclusion about not regretting decisions.

## 7. (E) Inference

### Step 1: Identify the Question Type

The correct answer will be "strongly supported" by the information given, making this an Inference question.

### Step 2: Untangle the Stimulus

The stimulus discusses two groups of Panamanian natives called the Kuna. One group lives on the islands and one group lives on the mainland. Unlike the mainland Kuna, the island Kuna drink a lot of flavonoid-rich cocoa and happen to suffer less from high blood pressure.

### Step 3: Make a Prediction

While it may be extreme to claim an absolute cause-and-effect relationship, the correlation is hard to deny. The author is suggesting that the cocoa, while perhaps not entirely responsible, at least *partly* explains why the island Kuna have less blood pressure problems.

### Step 4: Evaluate the Answer Choices

**(E)** is correct, drawing a loose link ("tends to prevent") between the cocoa and the blood pressure.

**(A)** is not supported. While the mainland Kuna do not drink the same amount of cocoa, there is no indication that this is because it (or any other flavonoid-rich food) is unavailable.

**(B)** is not supported. The island Kuna might just drink the cocoa because it's delicious. The benefits could just be a welcome side effect.

**(C)** is a 180. If low blood pressure were genetic, that wouldn't explain why the mainland Kuna experience more high blood pressure issues.

**(D)** is Out of Scope. The information only compares the mainland Kuna to the island Kuna. There is no information, and thus nothing to infer, about other mainland citizens.

## 8. (A) Strengthen/Weaken (Evaluate the Argument)

### Step 1: Identify the Question Type

The question asks for something that would help *evaluate* the stated hypothesis. This is an Evaluate the Argument question, a common variation of Strengthen/Weaken questions. The correct answer will raise a question that, depending on how it's answered, can affect the validity of the argument. In short, it will question the author's assumption.

### Step 2: Untangle the Stimulus

For some reason, jurors are more likely to believe scientific evidence if they hear it in court than if they hear the *very same* evidence outside of court. Legal theorists argue that this is primarily because judges sift through evidence before trial and only allow credible evidence to be presented.

### Step 3: Make a Prediction

The assumption here is that jurors take the judge's decision into account when assessing credibility. The correct answer will question whether the judge has any role in their assessment.

### Step 4: Evaluate the Answer Choices

**(A)** correctly questions the assumption. If jurors know about the judge's role, then that adds evidence to connect the jurors and the judge. If jurors *don't* know about the judge's role, then the hypothesis falls apart. The jurors couldn't possibly be influenced by something they don't even know about.

**(B)** doesn't help. The hypothesis is that jurors are *primarily* influenced by the judge's choices. That could be valid whether other jurors were partially influential or not at all.

**(C)** is a Distortion. The hypothesis is about judging the credibility of the evidence itself, not the person presenting the evidence.

(D) doesn't help. The hypothesis is that jurors are *primarily* influenced by the judge's choices. That could still hold whether jurors use any personal scientific knowledge or not.

(E) is an irrelevant hypothetical. The argument is only about why jurors are more persuaded *in* court than *out* of court, regardless of situations involving conflicting information.

## 9. (E) Paradox

### Step 1: Identify the Question Type

The correct answer will *explain* something *surprising*, making this a Paradox question.

### Step 2: Untangle the Stimulus

A study shows that word-of-mouth marketing is more effective when the person promoting a product admits they're part of a marketing campaign. This is surprising because the supposed benefit of word-of-mouth marketing is that it avoids the kind of skepticism raised by mass advertising.

### Step 3: Make a Prediction

It makes sense that people would trust a friend's recommendation over a random mass-marketing ad. Friends want to help us. Companies want to make money. However, once a friend or acquaintance says, "Oh by the way, I'm being paid to promote this product," you would expect skepticism to creep back in. But the study says otherwise. Why would people be *more* successful when admitting affiliation? There must be something about the openness and honesty that removes doubt and alleviates lingering concerns that the friend is hiding something. The correct answer will align with this concept of beneficial honesty.

### Step 4: Evaluate the Answer Choices

(E) helps. This suggests that honesty relaxes the customer, allowing the customer to be more open and less skeptical.

(A) is Out of Scope. The mystery is not about word-of-mouth versus mass-media ads. The mystery is about word-of-mouth with affiliations revealed versus word-of-mouth *without* affiliations revealed.

(B) is Out of Scope. The mystery revolves around why openly admitting affiliation is more effective than not admitting it. How the people "most receptive to mass-media marketing campaigns" act is irrelevant.

(C) doesn't help. It doesn't matter how the word-of-mouth campaigners got their jobs. It matters how well they *do* their job and whether admitting their affiliation helps.

(D) is Out of Scope. The cost of the campaigns is irrelevant to the effectiveness of openly admitting one's affiliation.

## 10. (D) Assumption (Sufficient)

### Step 1: Identify the Question Type

The question asks for something *assumed* by the argument, and the conclusion is said to be logically drawn *if* that assumption is made. That makes this a Sufficient Assumption question.

### Step 2: Untangle the Stimulus

The consultant concludes ([*t*]*herefore*) that Whalley will win the election by sticking with her current platform. According to the evidence, with her current platform, she'll lose with younger voters, but win by a bigger margin with older voters.

### Step 3: Make a Prediction

The issue here is one of numbers versus percentages. A greater percentage of votes from the 50-and-over crowd would be great, as long as there aren't substantially more under-50 voters. If there were 100,000 younger voters but only 1,000 older voters, the percentages would be misleading. In that case, losing the younger vote 51%–49% would put her down 2,000 votes. Thus, no margin of victory with older voters could help her win the election. For this argument to work, the consultant assumes that the total number of 50-and-over voters is large enough to compensate for the loss in the under-50 crowd.

### Step 4: Evaluate the Answer Choices

(D) is correct. If there are more older voters overall, then a larger margin of victory with that group ensures her victory in the election.

(A) is irrelevant. The argument is not about getting the most votes possible. It's just about winning. And the lack of an alternative platform does not guarantee that her current platform will win.

(B) is Out of Scope. The argument is based on numbers and whether the current poll numbers are indicative of a win for Whalley. The actual issues have no bearing on the argument.

(C) is irrelevant. The argument is based on Whalley sticking with her platform. What would happen if she changes does nothing to validate the conclusion.

(E) is irrelevant. The argument is about whether she could win with her current platform. It doesn't matter what would happen if she changed the platform. The consultant is not arguing about what would give Whalley the best chance of winning.

## 11. (E) Principle (Identify/Inference)

### Step 1: Identify the Question Type

The correct answer will be a generalization, making this an Identify the Principle question. In an unusual twist, the correct answer will be a principle that is *incompatible* with the given claims. That means it is similar to an Inference question that asks for a "must be false" answer.

### Step 2: Untangle the Stimulus

The stimulus compares Britain in 2000 to Britain in 1880. In 2000, the economy was much larger, while carbon dioxide emissions, per capita, were the same.

### Step 3: Make a Prediction

The correct answer will be incompatible with this data. The figures show that economic growth essentially has no effect on per capita carbon dioxide emissions. The correct answer will likely express the opposite: that economic growth *does* affect carbon dioxide.

### Step 4: Evaluate the Answer Choices

**(E)** is the correct answer. The stagnant carbon dioxide emission levels clearly show that economic growth does not *always* and *inevitably* increase emissions per person.

**(A)** is Extreme. The figures only show data from 1880 and 2000—nothing in between. It's possible that emissions decreased at *some* point in that 120-year span (while the economy grew), and then came back up by 2000.

**(B)** is Out of Scope. There is nothing in the stimulus about laws or the ability to afford such laws. And Britain's economy quintupled—which can hardly be described as "growing slowly or not at all."

**(C)** is a 180. This suggests that, as the economy grew, emissions could have increased at first then come back down. That's consistent with the emissions being the same in 1880 as they are in 2000.

**(D)** is Out of Scope. The stimulus doesn't mention population, so there's no incompatibility. Even if one assumes the real-life increase in population, this refers to *total* emissions *worldwide*. The consistency of *per capita* emissions in *Britain* would not necessarily conflict with that.

## 12. (B) Assumption (Necessary)

### Step 1: Identify the Question Type

The question directly asks for an assumption, and one "required by the argument." That makes this a Necessary Assumption question.

### Step 2: Untangle the Stimulus

The advertisement concludes ([c]*learly*) that it is always worth asking a lawyer for advice when writing a will. The reason is that, despite being more expensive than a do-it-yourself will-writing program, lawyers can tailor a will to fit your personal needs.

### Step 3: Make a Prediction

It would certainly be worthwhile if the lawyer provides something that do-it-yourself software doesn't. The

advertisement mentions that lawyers provide customization, but never actually says that do-it-yourself software *doesn't*. In order for this argument to work, it must be true that do-it-yourself software doesn't offer the same level of customization that a lawyer does.

### Step 4: Evaluate the Answer Choices

**(B)** is correct. Using the Denial Test, if the software *can* tailor a will as well as a lawyer can, then the author has no argument why a lawyer is *always* worth the extra expense. The author must assume that the software cannot tailor a will as well as a lawyer.

**(A)** is an Irrelevant Comparison. The author refers to doctors as an analogy. There is no need to make any comparison between lawyers and doctors. Even if a lawyer's knowledge were *less* complex than a doctor's, it could still be complex enough to warrant giving advice for drafting a will.

**(C)** is not necessary. Even if a lot of people are unsatisfied with do-it-yourself software, there could still be plenty of people who *are* satisfied. That wouldn't warrant the conclusion that lawyers are *always* worth the expense.

**(D)** is not necessary. How often wills adequately serve their purpose has no bearing on the issue of lawyer versus do-it-yourself program. It's also unclear from **(D)** whether those inadequate wills were prepared by an attorney or by do-it-yourself software. So, it's not even something that necessarily strengthens the advertisement either.

**(E)** is a Faulty Use of Detail. Doctors were only brought up as an analogy. The argument is ultimately about wills and lawyers. Whether people can or can't get a prescription without a consultation has no effect on the author's argument.

## 13. (A) Parallel Reasoning

### Step 1: Identify the Question Type

The correct answer will be an argument that is "most similar" in reasoning to the argument in the stimulus. That makes this a Parallel Reasoning question.

### Step 2: Untangle the Stimulus

The author concludes ([*s*]*o*) that indifference results in harm to nature's balance. That's because indifference leads to pollution, which in turn results in harm to nature's balance.

### Step 3: Make a Prediction

This argument is a straightforward connection of Formal Logic.

Evidence:

| If | X (indifference) | $\rightarrow$ | Y (pollution) |
|----|------------------|---------------|---------------|
| If | Y (pollution) | $\rightarrow$ | Z (harm balance) |

Conclusion:

> *If*    *X (indifference)*    →    *Z (harm balance)*

The correct answer will follow the same basic format.

**Step 4: Evaluate the Answer Choices**

**(A)** matches.

> *If*    *X (chocolate)*    →    *Y (high in calories)*
>
> *If*    *Y (high in calories)*    →    *Z (fattening)*
>
> *If*    *X*    →    *Z*

**(B)** does not match. It starts with:

> *If*    *X (chocolate)*    →    *Y (high in calories)*

But then the second sentence goes backwards:

> *If*    *Z (fattening)*    →    *Y (high in calories)*

Those claims cannot be combined the same way as the original because the Y term is necessary in both pieces of evidence. Also, in this argument, the conclusion is flawed due to improperly chaining the statements.

**(C)** does not match. It starts with:

> *If*    *X (high in calories)*    →    *Y (chocolate)*

But the second claim again starts with X:

> *If*    *X (high in calories)*    →    *Z (fattening)*

Those claims cannot be combined the same way as the original because the X term is sufficient in both pieces of evidence. Also, in this argument, the conclusion is flawed due to improperly chaining the statements.

**(D)** does not match even though the evidence is perfect.

> *If*    *X (chocolate)*    →    *Y (high in calories)*
>
> *If*    *Y (high in calories)*    →    *Z (fattening)*

But then the conclusion illogically reverses the logic...

> *If*    *Z*    →    *X*

... which is not what the original argument did.

**(E)** does not match. The evidence and the conclusion discuss "many desserts," which is not the same absolute logic as the original.

### 14. (C) Role of a Statement

**Step 1: Identify the Question Type**

The question provides a claim from the stimulus and asks for its "role in the argument," making this a Role of a Statement question. Start by marking the claim in the stimulus. Then look for the evidence and conclusion, and determine how the claim in question fits within that argument.

**Step 2: Untangle the Stimulus**

The argument concerns a school of thought called mechanism. In the 17th century, proponents produced a lot of arguments promoting mechanism. Some have theorized that so many arguments indicated a clash with democracy. *But* the author disagrees, concluding that that mechanism *supported* democracy. There were just so many arguments because they didn't work.

**Step 3: Make a Prediction**

The claim in question is what has been *construed* by others. The [*b*]*ut* in the following sentence indicates that the author argues *against* that claim. It's easy to get lost in all the philosophical jargon. However, the content is not all that important. What matters here is the structure. The claim in question is what some people believe, and the author goes on to refute that claim. That's its role within the argument.

**Step 4: Evaluate the Answer Choices**

**(C)** is correct. The contrast Keyword [*b*]*ut* is indicative of something the author *challenges*.

**(A)** is a 180. The author seeks to *contradict* the claim in question, not *establish* it.

**(B)** is a Distortion. The author seems to *contradict* the claim in question, not *explain* it.

**(D)** is a 180. The conclusion goes *against* the claim in question. The claim certainly does not support the conclusion.

**(E)** is not correct because the conclusion is the last sentence of the stimulus.

### 15. (C) Flaw

**Step 1: Identify the Question Type**

The question asks why the argument is *flawed*, making this a Flaw question.

**Step 2: Untangle the Stimulus**

The author concludes that Ishiko must be a good manager. The evidence is that Ishiko can defuse tension, and defusing tension (along with understanding people) is needed to be a good manager.

**Step 3: Make a Prediction**

This is a classic case of confusing necessity with sufficiency. Look at the stimulus in Formal Logic terms. According to the first sentence, if one is a good manager, then that person must understand people and be able to defuse tension:

> *If*    *good manager*    →    *understand people AND defuse tension*

The next piece of logic says that anyone who can defuse tension must understand people. So, if one can defuse tension, then that person can also understand people:

**If    defuse tension    →    understand people**

It is given that Ishiko can defuse tension. By the second piece of evidence, she must also be able to understand people. She now meets the requirements for a good manager, as presented in the opening sentence. However, those skills are merely *necessary*. They do not guarantee (i.e., they are not *sufficient* to know) that she is a good manager. The author makes that mistake, treating the necessary skills as if they were sufficient.

## Step 4: Evaluate the Answer Choices

**(C)** accurately describes this commonly tested LSAT flaw.

**(A)** is a Distortion. By the second piece of logic, defusing tension is a quality that is sufficient to show an understanding of people. However, the author never treats defusing tension as necessary for understanding people. It's said to be necessary for being a good manager, but the author doesn't even get *that* right, treating it as sufficient.

**(B)** is a Distortion. Defusing tension is not a quality that *correlates* with being a good manager. It's a quality that is necessary (i.e., *must* be present) to be a good manager. And the author doesn't say it "results from" being a good manager. The author suggests that it *causes* Ishiko to be a good manager, or at the very least is sufficient to indicate that she's a good manager.

**(D)** is irrelevant. *How* managers defuse tension has no bearing on the argument. The only issue is if they can or not.

**(E)** is a Distortion. The author does make an assumption about a quality (defusing tension) that all good managers have. However, the author is not *assuming* Ishiko must have that quality. That's already known. The assumption is that having that quality *makes* her a good manager.

## 16. (B) Paradox

### Step 1: Identify the Question Type

The question asks for something that would help *explain* some "strange behavior." That makes this a Paradox question.

### Step 2: Untangle the Stimulus

The stimulus describes a species of bird call a babbler. They live in large groups and make barking calls to each other when predators are nearby. However, they usually blend in very well and go unnoticed. The predators only see them when they start barking, and the barking continues long after they've found a good hiding spot.

### Step 3: Make a Prediction

The stimulus of a paradox usually boils down to a central mystery. In this case, if they're usually not seen by predators when they stay quiet, why do the babblers draw attention to themselves with so much barking? The correct answer will solve this mystery, likely offering a benefit of the barking that outweighs the attention it brings from predators.

### Step 4: Evaluate the Answer Choices

**(B)** explains the barking. Instead of taking the risk that their camouflage will get detected, they gather up an army of their friends, which will help intimidate and drive away the predator.

**(A)** does not help. If they could just fly away fast enough, it makes no sense to suddenly start barking and give away their location.

**(C)** does not help. They have camouflage, so it doesn't matter how many types of predators they have. The camouflage should be enough to keep them quiet.

**(D)** may be tempting, but the stimulus already states that the babblers are "extremely well camouflaged" and can usually go "unnoticed by predators." And predators realize the babblers are present "only because of their shrill barks." That suggests that, even with good eyesight and relatively weak hearing, the predators' eyesight still isn't good enough to recognize babblers through their camouflage, and their hearing isn't too weak to hear babblers' barks.

**(E)** is Out of Scope. The presence of other prey in the area does nothing to explain the babblers' behavior.

## 17. (A) Role of a Statement

### Step 1: Identify the Question Type

The question provides a claim from the stimulus and asks how it "figures in the argument." That makes this a Role of a Statement question. Mark the claim first. Then break the argument into evidence and conclusion, and consider how the marked claim fits within the context of the argument.

### Step 2: Untangle the Stimulus

According to the author, photographs of Europa suggest that there is a warm sea beneath the ice. As a second piece of evidence, the author says seas are important for life to develop. *So*, the author concludes that there may very well be life on Europa.

### Step 3: Make a Prediction

The claim in question is that there is a warm sea beneath Europa's icy surface. That is a conclusion based on the photographic evidence. However, it is not the ultimate conclusion. The author goes further and uses this claim as evidence, along with a second piece of evidence (seas are a factor in the development of life) for the main conclusion:

there may be life on Europa. So, the claim in question is merely a subsidiary conclusion, one that ultimately backs up the main conclusion.

**Step 4: Evaluate the Answer Choices**

**(A)** is correct.

**(B)** is incorrect because the main conclusion is the last sentence: there may be life on Europa.

**(C)** is Out of Scope. There is no theory being discredited or disputed.

**(D)** is Extreme. The author also raises the consideration that seas are "a primary factor in the early development in life." That other consideration, along with the claim in question, is presented in support of the conclusion.

**(E)** is incorrect. The claim itself is the subsidiary conclusion. The only thing the claim supports is the main conclusion.

## 18. (C) Main Point

**Step 1: Identify the Question Type**

The question asks for the "overall conclusion," which makes this a Main Point question.

**Step 2: Untangle the Stimulus**

Retailers like to take advantage of the fact that consumers enjoy feeling lucky. [*B*]*ut* the author argues that retailers use price-cutting tactics a bit too much. As evidence, the author claims that such promotions ultimately affect profits and hurt customer loyalty.

**Step 3: Make a Prediction**

Most of the argument consists of facts, and indisputable facts serve as evidence. Conclusions are opinions, and the author's opinion is only seen once in this argument: "too often." That makes that claim the main point: retailers too often use price cuts to promote their wares. Everything after that is evidence to support this opinion.

**Step 4: Evaluate the Answer Choices**

**(C)** correctly identifies the conclusion.

**(A)** is how consumers feel, not the author.

**(B)** is a given fact, not the conclusion. The conclusion comes right after this claim, where the author uses *but* to address a perceived problem.

**(D)** is the evidence in the last sentence that supports the author's conclusion. It helps prove *why* using those cuts too frequently is a bad idea.

**(E)** is a Distortion. The author is not disputing the idea of making customers feel lucky. The author is just disputing the overuse of price cuts as a way to do so.

## 19. (B) Role of a Statement

**Step 1: Identify the Question Type**

The question provides a claim from the stimulus and asks how it "functions in the argument." That makes this a Role of a Statement question. Start by marking the claim in question. Then, after breaking the argument into evidence and conclusion, consider how that claim fits within the argument.

**Step 2: Untangle the Stimulus**

The jurist claims it is important for legal systems to avoid giving unfair advantages to lawbreakers. *Thus*, the jurist concludes that the legal system should make sure criminals can't profit from their crimes.

**Step 3: Make a Prediction**

There are only two sentences in this argument. The second sentence is the conclusion. The first sentence (which contains the claim in question) is the supporting evidence. The correct answer will identify the first sentence as supporting evidence for the conclusion.

**Step 4: Evaluate the Answer Choices**

**(B)** is correct. The first claim is a principle (i.e., a general rule), and it does support the conclusion.

**(A)** is a Distortion. The condition raised in the claim is said to be important for the system to remain just. That suggests that it is *necessary*, but not a guarantee that ensures justice (i.e., it is *not sufficient* for justice).

**(C)** is incorrect. The second sentence is the conclusion. The claim in question is merely evidence.

**(D)** is Extreme. The author merely concludes what the legal system "should certainly attempt." The author never claims that this is the "most important goal."

**(E)** is Out of Scope. The author is not refuting anything.

## 20. (C) Assumption (Sufficient)

**Step 1: Identify the Question Type**

The question directly asks for what is *assumed* by the author, and the argument will be valid *if* that assumption is made. That makes this a Sufficient Assumption question.

**Step 2: Untangle the Stimulus**

The author concludes that a particular contract was violated. The contract in question requires that the company president or a lawyer in the legal department be notified of any changes. However, changes were made *without* notifying the president or Yeung.

**Step 3: Make a Prediction**

According to the evidence, changes need to be run by the president *or any lawyer in the legal department*. It is only mentioned that the president and Yeung (whoever that is) were unaware of the changes. If any one of the legal department's lawyers were told of the changes, then the rules were followed. To claim a violation, the author assumes that the legal department lawyers were *all* uninformed.

But what about Yeung? Yeung is a distraction here. Some might wonder: doesn't the author assume Yeung is one of the lawyers? In that case, the contract is violated, right? Not necessarily. Keep in mind that the contract requires notifying the president or *any* lawyer in the legal department. So, even if Yeung *was* one of those lawyers, that doesn't confirm that the contract was violated. There could still be other lawyers who *were* notified. This only works as an assumption if the author further assumes that Yeung is the *only* lawyer in the entire legal department.

### Step 4: Evaluate the Answer Choices

**(C)** is correct. If none of the lawyers were told about the changes, and the president wasn't told, then the contract was definitely violated.

**(A)** is not enough to guarantee the conclusion, as described in Step 3.

**(B)** is not enough. There is no information about who Grimes is, let alone Yeung. Even if they were both lawyers, there could still be other lawyers in the legal department. In that case, it's still possible that the contract was not violated.

**(D)** is a Distortion. What ensures that the contract is *not* being violated does nothing to confirm whether the contract *is* being violated. Adding **(D)** to the argument does not guarantee that the contract was violated; it's immaterial because the president was *not* told about the changes.

**(E)** is not enough. This is a valid inference based on the given evidence (because it's already known that the president was not informed). However, just setting up another conditional statement provides no evidence that the lawyers *were* uninformed. Without that information, there's still no guarantee that the contract was, indeed, violated.

### 21. (A) Strengthen

### Step 1: Identify the Question Type

The question directly asks for something that strengthens the given argument.

### Step 2: Untangle the Stimulus

The journalist concludes (*thus*) that eating less iron-rich food should reduce one's risk of Parkinson's disease. The evidence is that people with Parkinson's tend to have more iron in their diets.

### Step 3: Make a Prediction

This argument is based on implied causality. The author assumes that because people with Parkinson's happen to eat more iron-rich food, the iron-rich food is a *causal* factor. Thus,

eating less iron-heavy food will reduce the chances of it causing Parkinson's. However, causal arguments make three assumptions: 1) there's no alternative cause (i.e., the Parkinson's couldn't be spurred on by other foods), 2) the causality is not reversed (i.e., having Parkinson's does not cause people to eat more iron than usual), and 3) it's not a coincidence. The correct answer will validate one of these assumptions. In short, it will either eliminate an alternative cause, show how the causality is not reversed, or make a stronger connection between iron and Parkinson's.

### Step 4: Evaluate the Answer Choices

**(A)** strengthens the argument by implying that the causality is not reversed. If a genetic predisposition causes people to eat more iron, then the presence of iron is due to the disease itself. Reducing one's intake would not take away the disease. This suggests the opposite, that the genetic predisposition is irrelevant. That makes it more likely that iron is a catalyst for the disease (as the author suggests), and not the other way around.

**(B)** is a 180. This destroys the link between iron and Parkinson's, showing that some people with a lot of iron *don't* get the disease.

**(C)** is an Irrelevant Comparison. No distinction is made between younger and older people in the argument, and this comparison does nothing to connect iron to Parkinson's.

**(D)** is another Irrelevant Comparison. The author's conclusion is about a wholesale reduction of iron-rich foods, regardless of how easily the body absorbs the iron. This does nothing to confirm if that would help reduce the risk of Parkinson's.

**(E)** is Out of Scope. The author does not put an age limit on the recommendation, and this does nothing to confirm the link between iron and Parkinson's.

### 22. (E) Inference (EXCEPT)

### Step 1: Identify the Question Type

The correct answer will be logically determined based on a set of *statements*. That makes this an Inference question. However, this question contains an EXCEPT. Four of the answers (the wrong ones) all "could be true." The correct answer will be the exception—the one that must be false (i.e., the one that is impossible).

### Step 2: Untangle the Stimulus

The chairperson starts by comparing two candidates: Modernist Maples is a better candidate than Traditionalist Tannet. The chairperson then makes an even bolder claim: *every* Modern Party member would be better than *any* Traditionalist Party member.

### Step 3: Make a Prediction

In all, the comparison is merely between two parties. Anyone who is a member of the Modern Party is more qualified than anyone who is a member of the Traditionalist Party. The different members within each party may vary in quality, but even the worst member of the Modern Party will be more qualified than the best member of the Traditionalist Party. The correct answer will contradict that claim.

### Step 4: Evaluate the Answer Choices

**(E)** must be false and is thus correct. Tannet is a Traditionalist, and the chairperson is a Modernist. By the bold claim of the stimulus, the chairperson must be more qualified than Tannet, not the other way around.

**(A)** could be true because it is Out of Scope. The information only discusses qualifications, not *seniority*. Furthermore, even if Maples was in the Traditionalist Party before, he's not now, and the chairperson's claim did not extend to previous members of the parties—only current members. So, **(A)** is possible.

**(B)** could be true. Tannet is less qualified than any Modern Party member, but there is no way to know how Tannet compares to other members of the Traditionalist Party.

**(C)** could be true because it is Out of Scope. The question is only based on the chairperson's bold claims. There is no way to determine what other residents believe.

**(D)** could be true. There is no way to determine how Maples compares to other Modern Party members. All that matters is that, even if Maples *is* the worst Modern Party candidate, he is still better than any of those Traditionalist members.

### 23. (C) Strengthen/Weaken (Evaluate the Argument)

#### Step 1: Identify the Question Type

The question asks for a question that would help "evaluate the reasoning" given. That makes this an Evaluate the Argument question. The correct answer should question the assumption in a way that would strengthen or weaken the argument depending on the response.

#### Step 2: Untangle the Stimulus

The businessperson was late to a meeting today and blames parking lot maintenance. The evidence is that it took the businessperson 15 minutes to find a parking space, resulting in late attendance to the meeting.

#### Step 3: Make a Prediction

The timing cannot be denied. The businessperson was late because it took 15 minutes to find a parking space, and then whatever time to get from that spot to the building. However, was parking lot maintenance really to blame? The businessperson believes so, which assumes that those 15 minutes finding a space and getting from that space to the

building made all the difference. The correct answer will question whether 15 minutes is abnormally long or not.

#### Step 4: Evaluate the Answer Choices

**(C)** would help. If parking patterns usually allow for quick parking (say, 5–10 minutes), then the businessperson has a point—the maintenance created a delay. However, if parking patterns are usually terrible (i.e., it usually takes 15 minutes to find a spot), then the argument crumbles—the maintenance was irrelevant and thus *not* responsible.

**(A)** is Out of Scope. The reason for the maintenance has no bearing on whether it was responsible for the long search for a parking space.

**(B)** is irrelevant. If other people were late, it's still not certain whether the maintenance is to blame or if the company is just filled with people who normally arrive late. Maybe others were late because of a subway delay or because they slept in. If other people weren't late, it's still not certain if they commuted by another means of transportation or arrived at a time of day when more parking was available. Or maybe the maintenance issue was a factor, but they took more time to account for it, etc. **(B)** is not helpful in determining whether the businessperson's excuse is valid.

**(D)** is also irrelevant. Although it may be tempting to know the person's history, it really doesn't have bearing on this one occurrence. If the businessperson is usually on time, perhaps this was an exception. But is the maintenance to blame? This still doesn't help determine that.

**(E)** is irrelevant, too. The importance of the meeting has no bearing on why the businessperson was late.

### 24. (E) Inference

#### Step 1: Identify the Question Type

The correct answer will be a claim that the given statements "most strongly support," making this an Inference question. Even though the word *support* is in the question stem, this is not a Strengthen question. In a Strengthen question, the correct answer is used to support the argument in the stimulus. Here, as is typical in Inference questions, the order is reversed: the stimulus is used to support the correct answer.

#### Step 2: Untangle the Stimulus

The opening claim sets out what is required for a work to be called "world literature." It has to be interpreted within at least two traditions: that of the author's home country and that of an external nation. The author then presents three possible uses for a work that would allow it to be interpreted within a tradition: 1) to positively develop a tradition, 2) to negatively highlight something that should be avoided, and 3) to show something radical that inspires change.

## Step 3: Make a Prediction

There are a lot of abstract ideas here. Focus on the strongest points. The opening claim provides some Formal Logic. If a work is considered world literature, it must be interpreted within at least two traditions (the author's national tradition and an external national one):

| If | world literature | → | received/interpreted within writer's own national tradition AND received/ interpreted within external national tradition |
|----|------------------|---|--------------------------------------------------------------------------------------------------------------------------------|

By contrapositive, if it cannot be interpreted within those two traditions, then it's not really world literature. By the last sentences, there are numerous ways to achieve such an interpretation. While an exact answer will be difficult to predict, keep in mind two things. First, the two traditions are necessary, but not sufficient. Do not mix up the Formal Logic. Second, stick to the scope: what allows for traditional interpretation and what classifies a work as world literature.

## Step 4: Evaluate the Answer Choices

**(E)** is supported. If a work affects the development of only *one* tradition, then that allows only one interpretation. By the Formal Logic provided, that means it doesn't meet the requirement and thus cannot be considered world literature.

**(A)** is Out of Scope. The author never mentions anything about what makes a work "well received."

**(B)** is an Irrelevant Comparison. There's nothing to suggest which group of readers a work "offers more" to.

**(C)** is another Irrelevant Comparison. The requirement is just that the story be interpreted within both traditions. It does not matter whether one interpretation is "more meaningful" than the other.

**(D)** is Out of Scope. The author makes no mention of being "influenced by" other works.

## 25. (D) Parallel Flaw

### Step 1: Identify the Question Type

The question asks for an argument with reasoning "most similar" to that in the stimulus. Furthermore, that reasoning is described as *flawed*, making this a Parallel Flaw question. Find the flaw in the stimulus, and look for the answer that contains the exact same flaw.

### Step 2: Untangle the Stimulus

The author concludes ([*h*]*ence*) that there are more sociology majors than psychology majors in a particular class. The evidence is that most sociology majors are in the class and most psychology majors are not.

## Step 3: Make a Prediction

The problem here is a shift from percentages to numbers. More than 50% of sociology majors are in the class, and fewer than 50% of the psychology majors are. However, the *number* of students from each major depends on how many students there are in the first place. If there are 10 sociology majors but 100 psychology majors, then just 20% of psychology majors could be in the class (20), and that would automatically be more than all of the sociology majors. The correct answer will make the same mistake: it will provide evidence about two percentages and conclude that the group with the greater percentage has the greater *number*.

## Step 4: Evaluate the Answer Choices

**(D)** is a match. This provides evidence about two percentages (more than 50% of veggies at Valley Food and less than 50% of veggies at Jumbo Supermarket) and concludes that the group with the greater percentage has the greater number. Perhaps Valley Food only offers 3 different vegetables, 2 of which are organic, but the Jumbo Supermarket offers dozens of vegetables, 10 of which are organic.

**(A)** does not match. The two percentages are not used to make a faulty conclusion about one group having a greater number than the other.

**(B)** has a couple of flaws, but not the same flaw found in the stimulus. This provides evidence of a numeric comparison (one is more than another) and uses that to conclude what a percentage believes ("most Silver Falls residents must be in favor... "). It's possible that only a small number of residents were in favor of increased spending on either issue, which means although more prefer road spending than park spending, those that prefer road spending may not be a majority. Also, the conclusion indicates that most people are *against* spending on parks. Of those surveyed, it may not be their first choice for increased spending, but they may support increased spending for parks nonetheless. Flaws for sure, but not the same as in the stimulus.

**(C)** is flawed, but not because of its use of percentages. There's only one percentage. And if most trees fit a particular category (e.g., local), then that means more trees fit that category than any other. However, that's only true of the arboretum itself. It's flawed to extrapolate that information from the arboretum to the "San Felipe area" in general.

**(E)** is surely flawed, but for reasons that are very different from the original. This does shift from percentages in the evidence to numbers in the conclusion. However, the argument shifts scope from the percentages that have photos to the number of houses *on sale*. The original argument does not make that kind of improper shift in scope, so this is not a match.

### 26. (D) Weaken

#### Step 1: Identify the Question Type

The question directly asks for something that weakens the given argument.

#### Step 2: Untangle the Stimulus

The film director argues that the film studio is sure to recover the high production costs of the movie. Even if the movie itself doesn't earn enough money to cover the costs, the special effects technology being developed for the movie can be used on later films.

#### Step 3: Make a Prediction

The film director is taking a long-term perspective on the high production costs. If the film does well, the studio gets its money back. If the film fails, the studio can still make its money back by reusing the new technology to make other films. Unfortunately, the director only says that the technology *could* be used in later films. If for some reason the technology *doesn't* get used again, then the costs are sunk ... and so is the author's argument.

#### Step 4: Evaluate the Answer Choices

**(D)** weakens the argument. If technology used on unpopular films tends to be abandoned, then there *is* a risk of the studio losing money. The film could do poorly, and the technology budget would go to waste. The author's argument is shot.

**(A)** is a 180. If studios get to control the new technology, then they can use it as often as they need until they get their money back. That supports the director's assertion that the risk is minimal.

**(B)** is also a 180. If innovative special effects bring in huge crowds in general, then it's unlikely that this movie will be unpopular. That supports the idea that the risk of losing money is low.

**(C)** is irrelevant. The director already accounts for inadequate ticket sales. Even if this movie's ticket sales (no matter how good they are) don't offset the costs, the director maintains that the new technology could be reused on other films. The studio can still get its money back that way.

**(E)** is another 180. This is exactly what the director is banking on. If the current film doesn't do well, then the technology can be used to cut expenses on later films, allowing the technology costs to be recovered in the future.

# Section IV: Reading Comprehension
## Passage 1: Jury Nullification

| Q# | Question Type | Correct | Difficulty |
|---|---|---|---|
| 1 | Inference | E | ★ |
| 2 | Inference | D | ★ |
| 3 | Logic Reasoning (Parallel Reasoning) | C | ★ |
| 4 | Inference | D | ★ |
| 5 | Inference | E | ★★★ |
| 6 | Logic Reasoning (Method of Argument) | A | ★ |

## Passage 2: Sociohistorical Interpretations of Art

| Q# | Question Type | Correct | Difficulty |
|---|---|---|---|
| 7 | Global | B | ★★★ |
| 8 | Inference | C | ★ |
| 9 | Inference | E | ★ |
| 10 | Detail (EXCEPT) | D | ★ |
| 11 | Inference | C | ★★★★ |
| 12 | Logic Function | B | ★★★ |
| 13 | Logic Function | A | ★★ |
| 14 | Inference | E | ★ |

## Passage 3: Clay Tokens and the Evolution of Written Language

| Q# | Question Type | Correct | Difficulty |
|---|---|---|---|
| 15 | Global | A | ★★ |
| 16 | Inference | D | ★★★ |
| 17 | Detail | B | ★ |
| 18 | Detail | B | ★★ |
| 19 | Inference | C | ★★ |
| 20 | Inference | C | ★★★ |
| 21 | Inference | A | ★★★ |
| 22 | Logic Reasoning (Weaken) | B | ★★★★ |

## Passage 4: CFCs and the Ozone Layer

| Q# | Question Type | Correct | Difficulty |
|---|---|---|---|
| 23 | Detail | E | ★★ |
| 24 | Logic Reasoning (Strengthen) | A | ★★ |
| 25 | Inference | D | ★★★ |
| 26 | Logic Reasoning (Evaluate the Argument) | D | ★★★ |
| 27 | Inference | B | ★★★ |

# Passage 1: Jury Nullification

**Step 1: Read the Passage Strategically**

**Sample Roadmap**

| line # | Keyword/phrase | ¶ Margin notes |
|---|---|---|
| **Passage A** | | |
| 2 | disregard | Jury null.—override judge/facts |
| 3 | contrary | motives for null. |
| 9 | few; problems | causes problems |
| 10 | great | |
| 11 | First | |
| 12 | Because | 1) Juries don't explain reason |
| 13 | impossible | |
| 15 | evil | |
| 16 | rather than; good | |
| 17 | Second; insufficient | 2) Juries lack override |
| 21 | because; irrelevant | |
| 23 | Third; not | 3) Not the jury's job |
| 30 | Nevertheless | Auth: should disagree in public instead |
| **Passage B** | | |
| 35 | however | Police/prosec. can be overzealous |
| 36 | overzealous | |
| 38 | for example | juries can compensate |
| 43 | assisting | |
| 44 | both | Jury null. assists legislature when laws are broad |
| 47 | must | |
| 48 | settle | |
| 50 | unjust; useful | jury null. can indicate problems with laws |
| 52 | problem | |
| 55 | should ignore; but | Jury null. due to external factors rare |
| 56 | uncommon | |
| 60 | nevertheless | Need unanimous decision to nullify |
| 61 | appropriate | |

## Discussion

Passage A immediately introduces the **Topic**: jury nullification. This is when juries take matters into their own hands, regardless of the judge's instructions or the facts of the case. The author provides several reasons why juries do this (mercy for the defendant, dislike of the victim, civil disobedience), but complains that there are major problems with jury nullification. These problems are the **Scope** of the passage.

The next three paragraphs outline three such problems: 1) Juries don't have to explain their decisions, so there's no way to determine their motives. 2) Juries don't always have enough evidence to make such a decision. 3) It's not the jury's job to interpret or evaluate the laws; that's what legislators and judges are for.

In the final paragraph, the author of passage A argues that it's okay for jurors to disagree with the law, but such debates should be left out of the courtroom. The **Purpose** of passage A is to describe why jury nullification is bad. The **Main Idea** is that there are various problems with jury nullification.

Passage B has a different perspective. This author claims that police and lawyers can be overzealous in prosecuting criminals, and juries can offset such behavior. In the second and third paragraphs, the author discusses the **Topic** of jury nullification, with the **Scope** of discussing its advantages.

Paragraph 2 discusses how jury nullification can *help* legislatures by deciding what laws apply and what laws don't in certain cases. They do this because laws are often broadly worded to accommodate unexpected variations and competing views. Paragraph 3 mentions how jury nullification can send a signal that a particular law is problematic and unfair.

The author of passage B concedes that decisions could be based on factors that should be ignored, but argues this is rare. After all, nullification requires unanimous agreement among 12 people with diverse perspectives. The **Purpose** of passage B is to discuss the advantages of jury nullification. The **Main Idea** is that jury nullification can actually help legislatures and promote fairness.

The main relationship between these passages is that they take polar opposite views on the value of jury nullification. Passage A is all about the problems, while passage B sees a lot value in it.

## 1. (E) Inference

### Step 2: Identify the Question Type

The question asks for something the author of passage B *suggests*, making this an Inference question.

### Step 3: Research the Relevant Text

The question asks for a description of "some laws" that would justify jury nullification. Paragraph 2 of passage B discusses the nature of the laws themselves.

### Step 4: Make a Prediction

In lines 44–48, the laws that justify jury nullification are described as "general laws," created from the need "for broad language." The correct answer will describe this broad, general characterization.

### Step 5: Evaluate the Answer Choices

**(E)** is an exact match.

**(A)** is Out of Scope. While the laws may be fairly complicated, the author never states or directly suggests this.

**(B)** is Out of Scope. The author never describes the laws as out-of-date.

**(C)** is a Distortion. While some may consider general laws to be permissive, the author never directly addresses this quality as a reason for jury nullification.

**(D)** is Out of Scope. The author never describes laws as intruding on anything.

## 2. (D) Inference

### Step 2: Identify the Question Type

The question asks about the "attitude" of the author of passage B. Attitudes are not directly stated but are directly inferred from the author's language, making this an Inference question.

### Step 3: Research the Relevant Text

The attitudes of both authors are prevalent through the passages, so the entire text is relevant.

### Step 4: Make a Prediction

The difference in the authors' attitudes is stark. The author of passage A is highly critical of juries, suggesting that they could sometimes be using their power for "evil ends" (lines 14–16), and they could be acting on "insufficient evidence" (line 17). The author of passage B is more supportive, suggesting that juries are "assisting the legislature" (line 43) and performing "a useful function" (lines 50–51). The question asks about passage B's author, so the correct answer will describe that author's more accepting stance on what juries are doing.

### Step 5: Evaluate the Answer Choices

**(D)** matches the attitude of passage B's author.

**(A)** is a 180. The author of passage B approves of what juries are doing, which suggests a *more* trusting attitude.

**(B)** is Out of Scope. Neither author addresses the ability of jurors to "understand the laws."

(C) is Out of Scope and a 180 at worst. Only the author of passage A raises this concern. The author of passage B never addresses it and, if anything, would be *less* concerned given the author's more supportive stance.

(E) is Out of Scope. Passage B never addresses the concept of effecting social change.

## 3. (C) Logic Reasoning (Parallel Reasoning)

### Step 2: Identify the Question Type

The correct answer will be titles to two documents that indicate a relationship "most analogous" to that of passage A and passage B. That makes this akin to a Parallel Reasoning question from LR. Consider the relationship between passages A and B, and look for two titles that describe a similar relationship on a different topic.

### Step 3: Research the Relevant Text

Titles would reflect the main point of an entire passage, so all of the text is relevant. Instead, use the Purpose and Main Idea from Step 1.

### Step 4: Make a Prediction

The relationship between passages A and B is that passage A talks about the negatives of jury nullification, while passage B touts jury nullification as helpful. The correct answer will provide two titles that offer the same relationship on a different topic: the first indicating a discussion of problems, and the second indicating a discussion of how something is helpful.

### Step 5: Evaluate the Answer Choices

(C) matches the relationship. The first title refers to "inherent dangers," just as passage A talks about the problems of jury nullification. And the second title refers to how something can "assist the law," exactly as passage B does with jury nullification.

(A) is Half-Right, Half-Wrong. It brings up "pros and cons" in the second title, suggesting that passage B does the same. However, passage B only pushes the pros. The one con raised in passage B is immediately dismissed.

(B) may be tempting because the first title indicates "three central issues," which perfectly mimics the three problems brought up in passage A. However, the second title discusses "unexpected benefits," and passage B makes no suggestion that the benefits mentioned are *unexpected*.

(D) is Half-Right, Half-Wrong. While the second title fits, the first title mentions "troublesome history," which does not match passage A. Passage A never talks about the history of jury nullification.

(E) is Extreme. Even if it's implied, the author of passage A never directly argues for banning jury nullification. The bigger issue though is the second title, which mentions *inevitability*.

That does not match passage B, which only mentions that juries *can* use jury nullification in certain cases (lines 36–38).

## 4. (D) Inference

### Step 2: Identify the Question Type

The question asks for what the authors are "most likely to disagree over." That means it will not be directly stated, but will be directly supported by the information in the passages, making this an Inference question.

### Step 3: Research the Relevant Text

There are no content clues or line references, so the entire text of both passages is relevant.

### Step 4: Make a Prediction

To make a prediction here, it helps to consider the primary point at issue between both passages. The author of passage A argues that it's bad when juries take the law into their own hands. Passage B says that this is fine, and they actually *help* legislatures when they do that. The correct answer is likely to be consistent with this core disagreement.

### Step 5: Evaluate the Answer Choices

(D) is correct. The author of passage A says there are legislators and judges whose job is to interpret the law. It's *not* the jury's job (lines 23–28). The author of passage B suggests otherwise, saying that juries can use their "own discretion" (lines 37–38) to determine whether a law "should be applied to a particular defendant" (lines 41–43).

(A) is too one-sided. Only the author of passage A decries the fact that juries don't have to reveal their reasoning. Passage B offers no opinion on this subject, so disagreement cannot be logically inferred.

(B) is a 180. The author of passage A agrees that such scrutiny and debate is acceptable…. as long as it's done in public (lines 29–32). And the author of passage B also seems to favor scrutiny, suggesting it could be helpful.

(C) is Out of Scope. Passage A brings up elected officials, but never discusses any *bias* in their decisions. Passage B similarly does not discuss the issue of bias.

(E) is Out of Scope for passage A. Only passage B raises the issue of overzealousness on the part of police and prosecutors.

## 5. (E) Inference

### Step 2: Identify the Question Type

The question asks for what the author of passage A would be "likely to" say in response to a claim in passage B. There will be no directly stated response, but it will be backed up by what the author of passage A says, making this an Inference question.

**Step 3: Research the Relevant Text**

The claim passage B makes about jury nullification being justified occurs in lines 36–40. However, the support for a response by passage A's author would come from the problems raised in paragraphs 2–4.

**Step 4: Make a Prediction**

The author of passage A has three problems with jury nullification. The question is: which one would dispute the claim that juries are justified in deeming a case too trivial? The first problem (paragraph 2) involves juries not revealing their motives. That doesn't really apply here. The second problem (paragraph 3) raises concerns about insufficient evidence. That could certainly apply here. The author of passage A could argue that juries are not justified because they don't have all the facts.

The third problem (paragraph 4) is also a potential reason—the author of passage A could argue that juries are not justified because it's not their job to make that decision. The correct answer will address one of the two plausible arguments.

**Step 5: Evaluate the Answer Choices**

**(E)** is correct. Passage A directly discusses how "juries often have insufficient evidence to make a reasoned nullification decision" (lines 17–18).

**(A)** is irrelevant. While the author of passage A does admit that "instances of jury nullification are probably few" (lines 8–9), the rarity of such cases has no bearing on whether juries are *justified* in making such a decision.

**(B)** is Out of Scope. The author of passage A makes no mention of prosecutors presenting cases, nor what appearance such presentations would give.

**(C)** is Out of Scope. The author of passage A does not address the likelihood of agreement among jurors. Besides, if juries are not in accord, then jury nullification wouldn't happen, as it requires unanimous consensus (lines 57–61). The question is about whether juries are justified when they *do* make that decision.

**(D)** is a Distortion. The author of passage A could argue that this is not the jury's responsibility (as discussed in lines 23–28), but that doesn't mean jurors lack the *expertise*.

## 6. (A) Logic Reasoning (Method of Argument)

**Step 2: Identify the Question Type**

The question asks for the *relationship* between both passages. The answers describe *how* the authors present their material and *how* they relate. Finding *how* arguments proceed is the hallmark of a Method of Argument question.

**Step 3: Research the Relevant Text**

The relationship is defined by the passages as a whole, so all of the text is relevant.

**Step 4: Make a Prediction**

The relationship between the passages boils down to their opposing Main Ideas on jury nullification. Passage A describes the problems with jury nullification, while passage B supports it by pointing out its usefulness. The correct answer will focus on this discrepancy.

**Step 5: Evaluate the Answer Choices**

**(A)** is a match.

**(B)** is Out of Scope for passage B, which never discusses *improvements* to jury nullification.

**(C)** is Out of Scope. Neither passage focuses on "jury behavior."

**(D)** is part Distortion, part Out of Scope. Passage A does describe problems with jury nullification, but never suggests that they are *intractable* (i.e., hard to control). Further, passage B offers no solutions. Passage B just focuses on a more positive assessment of the same action.

**(E)** is Out of Scope. Passage A does not raise any questions.

# Passage 2: Sociohistorical Interpretations of Art

**Step 1: Read the Passage Strategically**

**Sample Roadmap**

| line # | Keyword/phrase | ¶ Margin notes |
|---|---|---|
| 3–4 | for example | Sociohistorical interp. art imposes class ideals |
| 8–9 | fail to clarify; however; two different ways | Auth: ignores that there are 2 different motives |
| 11 | first | 1. Art for display |
| 13 | For instance | 2. Art to mirror ideals |
| 16 | second | |
| 18 | like | |
| 20 | prefer | Auth: critics focus on 2nd motive |
| 21 | because | Make 2 assumptions |
| 25 | however; must | |
| 28 | must also | |
| 31 | Historically | Two classes commission art |
| 35 | not always | Tastes not prone to great art |
| 39 | interested largely | |
| 40 | obsessed | |
| 41 | As a result | |
| 44 | for example | |
| 45 | Moreover; against | Much art anti-elite ideals |
| 47 | unwillingly; misgivings; Because | Critics must assume ideals there, but hidden |
| 49 | must | |
| 50 | claim | |
| 52 | disapproved | |

## Discussion

The passage opens up with the **Topic**: sociohistorical interpretations of art. Critics who take this view (including Richard Taruskin, who is mentioned frequently throughout the passage) suggest that art merely reflects the ideals of the dominant or governing class. With the contrast Keyword *however*, the **Scope** becomes clear: there are problems with such an interpretation. It also sets up the **Purpose**: to criticize sociohistorical interpretations.

In paragraph 2, the author discusses two reasons art was produced for the elite. The first was for display—a chance for the elitist to say, "Hey, look at my house! I paid a really famous architect to make it for me. See how great my tastes are?" The second was to promote the elitist's personal ideals.

In paragraph 3, the author mentions that sociohistorical critics focus only on the second motive, as it conveniently fits their idea of art reflecting the ideals of the elite. Once again, the author interrupts with *however*, exposing two assumptions these critics make. First, they assume that the elite even *had* agreed-upon ideals they wanted to convey. Second, they assume that artists would never pervert the system for their own reasons.

The last two paragraphs present evidence that directly questions those two assumptions. By questioning those assumptions, the author's **Main Idea** is confirmed: art is not just about reflecting the ideals of the elite, as sociohistorical critics would suggest.

Paragraph 4 attacks the first assumption by showing how art was usually commissioned by two classes: aristocrats and the wealthy middle class. Neither of these groups exhibited high-minded ideals that enduring art would embody. Paragraph 5 attacks the second assumption, suggesting that the elite were unwillingly supporting art that actually went *against* their ideals. To maintain their view, sociohistorical critics would have to use some elaborate analysis to show that art actually *does* support elite ideals, just in hidden ways.

## 7. (B) Global

### Step 2: Identify the Question Type

This is a Global question because it asks for the "main point of the passage."

### Step 3: Research the Relevant Text

Because this is a Global question, the entire passage is relevant.

### Step 4: Make a Prediction

The Main Idea from Step 1 provides an adequate prediction: art is not just about reflecting the ideals of the elite, as sociohistorical critics would suggest.

### Step 5: Evaluate the Answer Choices

**(B)** is correct. It calls the sociohistorical interpretation "overly simplistic," suggesting that there's more to art than what they claim.

**(A)** is too narrow. It is a Faulty Use of Detail, focusing only on details from paragraph 4. This ignores the sociohistorical view and the author's criticism of that view.

**(C)** might be implied by some of the details in paragraph 2, but completely misses the point of the entire passage regarding the sociohistorical interpretation of art.

**(D)** is too narrow. It is a Faulty Use of Detail, focusing only on the one problem raised in the last paragraph. This ignores the other assumptions raised and questioned in preceding paragraphs.

**(E)** is also too narrow and a Faulty Use of Detail. It mentions a detail raised at the end of the first paragraph and explained in the second paragraph. However, that's just one step on the author's path to the bigger picture: a wholesale criticism of sociohistorical interpretation.

## 8. (C) Inference

### Step 2: Identify the Question Type

The question asks what the author "most probably means" by a certain phrase. That meaning will not be stated directly but will be directly implied, making this an Inference question.

### Step 3: Research the Relevant Text

The question points to lines 12–13. The example that follows in lines 13–16 helps provide a better understanding of the author's meaning.

### Step 4: Make a Prediction

The author is discussing how some members of the elite commissioned art "for display." As an example, the author mentions hiring a famous architect to build a house, even one that is impossible to live in, all for the purpose of reflecting "great credit on one's taste." In other words, it's all about showing off and making a good impression.

### Step 5: Evaluate the Answer Choices

**(C)** matches the implied self-centered meaning.

**(A)** is a Faulty Use of Detail. The idea of *display* is part of the *first* motive presented in the paragraph. Making political statements (or expressing ideals) is part of the *second* motive.

**(B)** is Out of Scope. There's no mention of or suggestion of attracting customers to a business. In fact, the example provided is about a home, not a business.

**(D)** is Out of Scope. The creation of "something for display" reflects the member of the elite who commissioned the art, not the artist who created it.

**(E)** is a 180. As the example shows, it's all about reflecting credit on one's taste, even if one is *not* satisfied with the final product. ("What do you mean I can't live there?!?")

### 9. (E) Inference

#### Step 2: Identify the Question Type

The question asks for an *attitude* that can be *inferred* from the passage, making this an Inference question.

#### Step 3: Research the Relevant Text

Matthew Arnold's views are presented in lines 36–41.

#### Step 4: Make a Prediction

Arnold uses some harsh words to describe the two classes. He calls aristocrats *Barbarians* and mocks the middle class as "obsessed with respectability." The correct answer will be a word that describes this derisive attitude.

#### Step 5: Evaluate the Answer Choices

**(E)** works perfectly.

**(A)** is a 180. Name-calling is hardly a sign of respect.

**(B)** is Out of Scope. There's no indication that Arnold shares their feelings.

**(C)** is a 180. If Arnold didn't care, he likely wouldn't resort to cheap attacks.

**(D)** is a Distortion. Arnold certainly has a negative attitude, but "disappointment" suggests that he expected better. ("Oh, aristocrats—you could have been so much more!")

### 10. (D) Detail (EXCEPT)

#### Step 2: Identify the Question Type

The question asks for issues directly raised in the passage, making this a Detail question. Furthermore, this is an EXCEPT question, which means the correct answer will be the one detail that is *not* found in the passage.

#### Step 3: Research the Relevant Text

Complications primarily begin in paragraph 3, but are found throughout all of the last three paragraphs.

#### Step 4: Make a Prediction

It's impossible to predict something that is *not* in the passage, but a quick reminder of the major complications can help efficiently eliminate the wrong answers, which all *are* in the passage. Paragraph 4 raises the question of patrons who lacked the kind of ideals that would inspire great art. And paragraph 5 raises the issue of artists who might actually create anti-establishment art unbeknownst to those paying for it. Start by eliminating answers that match these broader issues.

#### Step 5: Evaluate the Answer Choices

**(D)** is correct, as the passage never brings up the concept of "reselling…. artwork for a profit."

**(A)** is raised in lines 45–46, which mentions art that "went against the grain of elite values." This shows that artists *did* subvert the ideals of the patrons, contrary to the assumption raised in lines 28–30.

**(B)** is raised in lines 41–44. These eccentric patrons are "in the margins," not exactly aligned with the ideals suggested by the sociohistorical critics.

**(C)** is raised in lines 34–36 as a direct questioning of sociohistorical critics' assumptions.

**(E)** is raised in lines 45–47 as art that directly goes against the sociohistorical critics' view.

### 11. (C) Inference

#### Step 2: Identify the Question Type

The question asks for something the passage *suggests*, making this an Inference question.

#### Step 3: Research the Relevant Text

Taruskin is mentioned many times in the passage. However, it's only in the last paragraph (lines 47–52) that the author describes a view Taruskin is forced to accept ("must engage" in line 49).

#### Step 4: Make a Prediction

According to the last line, some anti-establishment art endured. Because of that, Taruskin has to believe that this art actually *supported* elite ideals, but did so in "hidden ways."

#### Step 5: Evaluate the Answer Choices

**(C)** matches the view expressed in the final sentence.

**(A)** is Extreme. Taruskin must believe there are works that embodied elite ideology in hidden ways, but it never says the artists who made such works were "the *most* talented artists throughout history."

**(B)** is Out of Scope. The passage is about historical art, not "artists working today." Besides, there's no discussion of the "most successful artists," a decisively Extreme concept.

**(D)** is unsupported. There's no suggestion as to which class the artists themselves belong.

**(E)** is an Extreme 180. It not only refers to the "most talented artists throughout history" (which is unwarranted by the language of the passage), but also talks only about subverting elite ideology. Taruskin's view is the *opposite*, suggesting that those works only *appear* to subvert the ideology, but actually support the ideology in hidden ways.

## 12. (B) Logic Function

### Step 2: Identify the Question Type

The question directly asks for the function of the third paragraph.

### Step 3: Research the Relevant Text

The purpose of paragraph 3 can best be identified by referring to the margin notes for that paragraph.

### Step 4: Make a Prediction

In paragraph 3, the author identifies the kind of art that fits the sociohistorical view. The author then describes what "must be the case" in order for "this kind of analysis to work." In other words, the author presents assumptions required by that view, which was introduced in the first paragraph.

### Step 5: Evaluate the Answer Choices

**(B)** is a match.

**(A)** is Out of Scope. The author does not reject anything in the third paragraph. The author only raises assumptions that are rejected in the *following* paragraphs.

**(C)** is inaccurate. The information in the second paragraph is never contradicted. The author merely mentions how critics look at only one side of the situation and ignore the other. Plus, this ignores the assumptions raised.

**(D)** is inaccurate. There is no conclusion in the second paragraph. It just outlines two ways art was commissioned.

**(E)** is Extreme. The author raises assumptions, but never reaches a "definitive conclusion."

## 13. (A) Logic Function

### Step 2: Identify the Question Type

The question asks for the *reason* a particular claim was made. That means asking *why* it was included, making this a Logic Function question.

### Step 3: Research the Relevant Text

The question points to lines 18–19, but consider the purpose of the entire paragraph and how it relates to the rest of the passage.

### Step 4: Make a Prediction

The second paragraph describes two ways art was produced for the elite. The Raphael frescoes are mentioned as an example of the second way (lines 16–19), which involves producing art that "expressed and mirrored one's ideals." The correct answer will certainly express this illustrative function, but consider how this relates to the rest of the passage, which concerns the sociohistorical critics. In the very next paragraph (lines 20–21), the author mentions how those critics prefer the method described in lines 16–19. So, the

frescoes are not just an example of any old method, but of the very one preferred by the critics.

### Step 5: Evaluate the Answer Choices

**(A)** is correct, citing the frescoes as an example that is consistent with the sociohistorical view.

**(B)** is a Distortion. While the Vatican is certainly a religious locale (and the art is said to be commissioned by a pope—a religious figure), it's just a setting for the example. The author does not express any ideas about religious influence.

**(C)** is Extreme. The author never claims either method discussed in the second paragraph is the *most* common.

**(D)** is a Faulty Use of Detail. The idea of subverting ideals is not mentioned until the end of the third paragraph and has no direct connection to Raphael's frescoes.

**(E)** is a 180. The frescoes are an example of the method that *does* fit the pattern preferred by the critics.

## 14. (E) Inference

### Step 2: Identify the Question Type

The question asks for something the passage *suggests* and that Matthew Arnold is "most likely to" claim. That indicates an Inference question.

### Step 3: Research the Relevant Text

The question asks about Matthew Arnold, whose views are raised at the end of the fourth paragraph. Further, it asks about people in the middle class, whom Arnold addresses in lines 40–41.

### Step 4: Make a Prediction

Arnold calls the middle class "Philistines, obsessed with respectability." So, if the middle class were patrons of the arts, Arnold would likely claim they were doing so to feed their obsession with gaining respect.

### Step 5: Evaluate the Answer Choices

**(E)** is a match.

**(A)** is not supported. Arnold says the middle class is "obsessed with respectability," not actually concerned with art or society as a whole.

**(B)** is Out of Scope. There's no mention of what kind of art the middle class liked or disliked. There's also nothing mentioned about the middle class's opinion of the aristocracy's artistic tastes.

**(C)** is Out of Scope. The author never discusses profit as a motive.

**(D)** is a 180 at worst. The middle class is said to have tastes that do *not* lend themselves to enduring art. Further, Arnold makes no mention of patronage ensuring "the production of high-quality art."

# Passage 3: Clay Tokens and the Evolution of Written Language

**Step 1: Read the Passage Strategically**

**Sample Roadmap**

| line # | Keyword/phrase | ¶ Margin notes |
|---|---|---|
| 3 | Though | Clay tablets: |
| 5 | instead | abstract symbols, not pictographs |
| 6 | for example | Older tokens |
| 7 | but | S-B says precursor to writing |
| 9 | Because of; seemingly sudden | |
| 10 | long puzzled | |
| 15 | Often ignored | |
| 16 | concluded; without evidence | |
| 19 | overlooked | |
| 30 | theorizes | • Early tokens simple<br>• clay envelopes had impressions of tokens<br>• S-B: envelope held records<br>• more industry → more tokens |
| 39 | replaced | Tokens replaced by marks on tablets |
| 41 | first | led to mature writing |
| 43 | eventual evolution | example |
| 45 | suggests; : | |
| 46 | At first | |
| 47 | a little later | |
| 51 | Eventually | |

## Discussion

The passage opens with the discovery of ancient clay tablets in which the writing consisted of abstract symbols instead of pictographs (i.e., pictures representing words). Researchers were surprised by such an early appearance of abstract writing. However, excavations have also uncovered a bunch of even older tokens, which one researcher (Denise Schmandt-Besserat) claims are precursors to the written word. It's this last sentence that sets up the **Topic** (clay tokens) and **Scope** (their role as precursors to writing) of the passage.

The second paragraph describes the tokens. The earliest ones were basic shapes, and lots of them were found along with clay envelopes. The tokens were used to indicate the contents, which Schmandt-Besserat claims were records of temple contributions made by villagers. Later tokens took more advanced shapes as villagers started creating a greater variety of more sophisticated crafts.

The third paragraph charts the evolution from tokens to actual writing. Over time, the tokens were replaced with marks on the envelopes, and these marks eventually added numerals to indicate amounts. And this is how writing developed, according to Schmandt-Besserat. The final half of the paragraph is just an extended example that illustrates this evolution. With no clear author's point of view, the **Purpose** of this passage was merely to describe the role of tokens and Schmandt-Besserat's theory. The **Main Idea** is that, according to Schmandt-Besserat, these tokens were used to indicate the content of clay envelopes and served as a precursor to the written word.

## 15. (A) Global

### Step 2: Identify the Question Type

The question asks for the "main point" of the passage, making this a Global question.

### Step 3: Research the Relevant Text

All of the text is relevant to this question. Instead, focus on the Main Idea of the passage, as discovered in Step 1.

### Step 4: Make a Prediction

The main point is devoid of any strong opinion. It all boils down to Schmandt-Besserat's theory that the tokens found within the clay tablets were a predecessor to the written word.

### Step 5: Evaluate the Answer Choices

**(A)** is correct.

**(B)** is Extreme. The author merely presents Schmandt-Besserat's views. Her views are never said to be *confirmed*.

**(C)** is Extreme and a Faulty Use of Detail. Nothing suggests that the envelopes and tokens were *required* to solve anything. And the archaeologists were puzzled about the appearance of abstract writing (lines 9–11), *not* the

appearance of "sophisticated crafts" (which were only brought up in lines 36–37).

**(D)** is a Distortion. The evidence indicated the tokens and inscriptions formed the basis for *writing*, not for "modern language"—which may imply both a written and oral component. Furthermore, the passage describes the evolution of the tokens into *one* ancient written language—not multiple modern *languages*. Finally, although the transition from clay tokens to markings on clay tablets may have shown the dawn of the written word, the passage does not indicate that Schmandt-Besserat had a "detailed picture of the way in which" this lead to *modern* languages.

**(E)** is Extreme and a Distortion. Again, Schmandt-Besserat's views are merely presented, never *confirmed*. Moreover, only the symbols on the tablets are said to be abstract, not the people's *language* or their *crafts*.

## 16. (D) Inference

### Step 2: Identify the Question Type

The question asks for something with which Schmandt-Besserat is "most likely to agree," which makes this an Inference question.

### Step 3: Research the Relevant Text

The question asks about Schmandt-Besserat's view on the society where tokens were used. These views are presented throughout the second and third paragraph.

### Step 4: Make a Prediction

The question is very vague, but stick to the basic concepts behind Schmandt-Besserat's views. In the second paragraph, she discusses how villagers made contributions to the temple, and tokens were used to indicate what they contributed. In the third paragraph, the society stopped using tokens, as they were easily replaced by marks on the tablets. The correct answer is hard to predict, but will be consistent with these ideas.

### Step 5: Evaluate the Answer Choices

**(D)** fits the scenario as described. Once the society realized you could just make a mark on an envelope to indicate its contents, the token was "replaced" by such marks (lines 38–40). There was no need for both the marks *and* the tokens.

**(A)** is not supported. Even if Schmandt-Besserat is right and the envelopes contained records of temple contributions, that's not necessarily an indication of a "strong centralized government authority."

**(B)** is an Irrelevant Comparison. The passage never brings up the importance of, or even the presence of, religious rituals.

**(C)** is Extreme. While Schmandt-Besserat's theory involves villagers contributing to a communal pool of grain and livestock, that is not to say that *anything* they made became the property of *everyone*.

**(E)** is a Distortion. The token just happened to be made of clay, but there's no reason to suggest they couldn't have been made of other materials in the absence of clay.

## 17. (B) Detail

**Step 2: Identify the Question Type**

The question asks for something the passage *states*, making this a Detail question.

**Step 3: Research the Relevant Text**

The writing on the tablets found in Uruk is described in lines 3–6.

**Step 4: Make a Prediction**

According to lines 3–6, the writing on the tablets from Uruk used "numerous abstract symbols" and "relatively few pictographs."

**Step 5: Evaluate the Answer Choices**

**(B)** is directly stated in line 5.

**(A)** is a Faulty Use of Detail. 1992 is when Schmandt-Besserat published her book on the tokens. There is no date given for when the Uruk tablets were deciphered.

**(C)** is a Distortion. It's the *tokens* described later in the passage that evolved into writing, not the Uruk tablets. Also, "linguistic system" is too general because it was just a written language—not oral—that the tokens gave rise to.

**(D)** it Out of Scope. There is no mention of languages "commonly spoken along the Jordan and nearby rivers."

**(E)** is a Distortion. The archaeologists were not surprised at the age of the language, they were surprised by how early such *writing* appeared.

## 18. (B) Detail

**Step 2: Identify the Question Type**

This question asks for something known about the token system "[a]ccording to the passage." That means it will be directly stated in the passage, making this a Detail question.

**Step 3: Research the Relevant Text**

The token system is described throughout the second paragraph.

**Step 4: Make a Prediction**

There are a lot of details about the token system throughout the second paragraph. It's not necessary to predict the exact detail the LSAT will select, but take quick stock of the basics: The tokens were used to indicate the contents of the envelopes. The original shapes were basic, but later shapes got more elaborate as the crafts became more sophisticated.

Look for anything consistent with these facts, and confirm that it is mentioned in the passage.

**Step 5: Evaluate the Answer Choices**

**(B)** is mentioned in lines 33–37.

**(A)** is a 180. The example provided in the last paragraph shows that tokens *could* represent quantity (lines 46–47). The tokens were replaced because it was just as easy to represent quantity through marks on the envelope.

**(C)** is Extreme. Schmandt-Besserat's theory in lines 28–33 was based on recognizing known symbols, but that doesn't mean it was *only* for that reason that the token system could be understood.

**(D)** is Out of Scope. There's no mention of anyone claiming the tokens had a religious function.

**(E)** is a Distortion. The tokens took new forms (lines 34–37), but were never said to become "unwieldy and cumbersome."

## 19. (C) Inference

**Step 2: Identify the Question Type**

The question asks what the author "most likely means" by using a particular term. This intended definition will be suggested by the context around the term, making this an Inference question.

**Step 3: Research the Relevant Text**

The question points directly to line 10, but the word *abstract* is used in a phrase that begins "this seemingly sudden appearance….," which refers to the example right before. That example describes the symbols for *sheep* (a circled cross) and *metal* (a crescent with five lines).

**Step 4: Make a Prediction**

Picture a circled cross. Then picture a crescent with five lines. Do those images look like sheep or metal? Not even close. These symbols look nothing like the words they represent. So, in calling the writing *abstract*, it means just that: it represents items but looks nothing like those items.

**Step 5: Evaluate the Answer Choices**

**(C)** fits the description of the *sheep* and *metal* symbols.

**(A)** is a Distortion. While the symbols don't *look* like sheep or metal, that doesn't necessarily mean they were "hard to decipher."

**(B)** is a 180. They represent *sheep* and *metal*, objects which are certainly tangible (i.e., can be physically touched).

**(D)** is a 180. While *metal* can be considered a general category, *sheep* is a fairly specific animal.

**(E)** is unsupported. Nothing suggests that these symbols were *ceremonial*, and there's no comparison made between these symbols and "most daily speech."

## 20. (C) Inference

### Step 2: Identify the Question Type

The question asks for something that can be *inferred*, making this an Inference question.

### Step 3: Research the Relevant Text

The question directly points to the second paragraph.

### Step 4: Make a Prediction

The second paragraph has a lot of information, so a lot can be inferred about the tokens. Just focus on some of the most prominent information: The tokens were used to indicate the contents of the envelopes. The original shapes were basic, but later shapes got more elaborate as the crafts became more sophisticated. Look for an answer that is consistent with these details and has direct support in the passage.

### Step 5: Evaluate the Answer Choices

**(C)** is supported. The early forms are described as just shapes, e.g., spheres and pyramids (lines 20–21), while later forms actually looked like something, e.g., bowls or jars with handles (lines 35–36).

**(A)** is not supported. There were many different tokens, so it's certainly possible that each token represented a different unique item. It's never suggested that any particular token represented more than one item.

**(B)** is not supported. While later tokens started to represent nonagricultural products, there is no suggestion that such products were "preferred as contributions."

**(D)** is Extreme and Out of Scope. There is no mention of what tasks were "most important." Besides, the second paragraph never even mentions liquids, let alone storage and transportation of them.

**(E)** is a Distortion and a Faulty Use of Detail. The evolution to written language is not brought up until the third paragraph. Further, the author never compares them and suggests equal abstractness or flexibility.

## 21. (A) Inference

### Step 2: Identify the Question Type

The question asks what the author is "most likely to agree" about, making this an Inference question.

### Step 3: Research the Relevant Text

The question refers to the *sheep* symbol mentioned in paragraph 1.

### Step 4: Make a Prediction

As described in lines 6–7, the symbol for *sheep* was just a circled cross. It didn't actually look like a sheep at all. That suggests a random choice. Anything would have been just fine; the Sumerians just settled on a circled cross.

### Step 5: Evaluate the Answer Choices

**(A)** is supported. Because the symbol didn't actually look like a sheep, it could just have easily been two dots and a triangle. The important thing was that everyone knew that it was supposed to mean sheep.

**(B)** is not supported. While the symbols look different (a circled cross vs. a crescent with five lines), the meaning appears to be derived the same way: just pick some random shapes and assign them meaning.

**(C)** is not supported. There's no evidence why a circled cross was used or how a circled cross would have any stronger connection to agriculture than to human industry.

**(D)** is not supported and is a Distortion. Schmandt-Besserat studied the tokens, not necessarily the Sumerian symbols. Plus, there's no evidence of when those symbols were initially studied, whether it was before or after Schmandt-Besserat's studies.

**(E)** is Out of Scope. There is no mention of "political life," and it's difficult to imagine how much a circled cross could actually reveal about such political life.

## 22. (B) Logic Reasoning (Weaken)

### Step 2: Identify the Question Type

The question asks for something that would "call into question" Schmandt-Besserat's reasoning. That makes this a Weaken question, like the ones found in the Logical Reasoning section.

### Step 3: Research the Relevant Text

The question directly points to the theory in lines 28–33. Be sure to also consider the evidence for that theory in the previous lines.

### Step 4: Make a Prediction

Schmandt-Besserat's theory is that the envelopes contained records of "villager's contributions to temple-based grain and livestock pools." The evidence is that the token impressions revealed inscriptions that matched known inscriptions of farm products. While grain and livestock are certainly farm products, there's nothing that suggests that these were being donated to temple-based community pools. Schmandt-Besserat overlooks any other type of transaction that might have involved those products. To weaken her theory, the correct answer will suggest that there may have been a *different* reason for recording quantities of farm products.

### Step 5: Evaluate the Answer Choices

**(B)** weakens Schmandt-Besserat's theory. If records were used to indicate an exchange of agricultural products for services (e.g., "Build me a fence and I'll give you two chickens"), then it's possible that the records discovered had nothing to do with contributions to a communal pool of agricultural goods.

**(A)** is irrelevant. Different sizes of the envelopes could just have indicated different quantities of contributions, different preferences of construction by the envelope-makers, or it could have just been coincidence that the envelopes varied. Schmandt-Besserat's theory holds just fine.

**(C)** is irrelevant. The tokens were used up until 3100 B.C. (lines 38–40). It's certainly possible that the older tablets were used to record temple-based contributions, while later tablets (after 3000 B.C.) were used for different purposes.

**(D)** is irrelevant. The evidence states that the envelopes were "inscribed with impressions of tokens," which suggests that it's perfectly plausible that the tokens were never actually placed inside the envelope. Furthermore, a lack of (archaeological) evidence is not evidence of absence. Remember your flaws from Logical Reasoning! So, this would not affect Schmandt-Besserat's theory at all.

**(E)** does not weaken her theory. While there may be *other* records that indicated labor, the envelopes discovered still showed symbols of agricultural products and so could still have been records of *those* contributions.

# Passage 4: CFCs and the Ozone Layer

**Step 1: Read the Passage Strategically**

**Sample Roadmap**

| line # | Keyword/phrase | ¶ Margin notes |
|---|---|---|
| 1 | well established | UV → skin cancer |
| 3 | Fortunately; most damaging | ozone protects |
| 7 | however | CFCs attack ozone |
| 8 | alerted to | chlorine devastating |
| 9 | pioneering | |
| 12 | should | |
| 19 | attack; deplete | |
| 20 | diminishing | |
| 22 | observed | |
| 28 | devastating | |
| 30 | both | |
| 31 | As a result | |
| 39 | even if | Lots of CFCs in atmosphere |
| 41 | pressing | M&R: need to take action |
| 42 | threat | |
| 44 | As a result | |
| 50 | attacks; especially | Critics at first |
| 51 | However | Evidence confirmed problem |
| 52 | especially | Anti-CFC policies adopted |
| 54 | led to | |
| 55 | ban | |
| 57 | banned; leading to | |

**Discussion**

The passage opens with some science. Ultraviolet (UV) light from the sun contributes to skin cancer. *Fortunately*, the Earth has a layer of ozone that protects us.

Unfortunately, that layer is under attack. According to scientists Molina and Rowland, the ozone layer is fragile and can be destroyed by chemicals known as CFCs. That would take away some of our protection from skin cancer.

In paragraph 3, Molina and Rowland discover that the atmosphere is filled with ozone-destroying CFCs, and the situation is only getting worse. This compels them to educate the public and advocate change.

Initially, there are skeptics—chiefly scientists making money in the CFC business, of course. However, Molina and Rowland get some powerful backup in the form of a *giant hole in the ozone layer*. That catches people's attention, leading to new laws and regulations banning and replacing CFCs.

There's a lot of potential here for getting buried under the weight of scientific jargon—chlorofluorocarbons, freon, troposphere, diffusion. However, when simplified, this passage boils down to a very basic structure. It's merely about the ozone layer (**Topic**) and its susceptibility to CFCs (**Scope**), and it was written to inform the reader (**Purpose**) that CFCs can destroy the helpful ozone layer. The efforts of scientists Molina and Rowland brought about changes to prevent that problem from getting worse (**Main Idea**).

**23. (E) Detail**

**Step 2: Identify the Question Type**

The correct answer will be a question that is directly answered somewhere in the passage. Because the answer to that question will be directly stated, this is a form of Detail question.

**Step 3: Research the Relevant Text**

The question provides no content clues, so all the text is relevant.

**Step 4: Make a Prediction**

Because the question can bring up anything from anywhere in the passage, there's no need to attempt to predict the correct answer. Instead, consider each answer one at a time, eliminating ones that ask about concepts outside the scope of the passage. Use the answer choices to do any necessary research, and make sure the question in the correct answer is directly answered in the passage.

**Step 5: Evaluate the Answer Choices**

**(E)** is answered in lines 24–31, which mentions chlorine as the element of CFCs that reacts with ozone "in a way that.... destroys the ozone" (lines 29–30).

**(A)** is never mentioned. While it is mentioned that Molina and Rowland did research, their actual experiments were never described.

**(B)** is never mentioned. The passage never brings up actual numbers. The closest figure is in lines 34–36, which mentions that the atmosphere had about five years' worth of CFCs. But that's not a concentration, and that was in 1974, not 1987.

**(C)** is never mentioned. Testifying before Congress was mentioned at the end of the third paragraph. That paragraph starts in 1974, but the testifying occurred "as a result" of the scientists' advocacy. That could have been any number of years later.

**(D)** is Out of Scope. The passage only discusses CFCs. While other such chemicals may very well exist, none of them are mentioned here.

**24. (A) Logic Reasoning (Strengthen)**

**Step 2: Identify the Question Type**

The question asks for something that would *strengthen* the scientists' argument, making this a Strengthen question like the ones found in Logical Reasoning.

**Step 3: Research the Relevant Text**

The long-term effects of CFCs, according to Molina and Rowland, are described in paragraph 3.

**Step 4: Make a Prediction**

In lines 36–41, Molina and Rowland conclude that the ozone layer would continue to be destroyed even if we stopped producing CFCs. This is based on evidence of the rate at which CFCs break down and the fact that there is five years' worth of CFCs in the atmosphere. The author assumes that nothing would change and CFCs would, indeed, continue to destroy the ozone layer after we stop production. The correct answer will be something that validates a continued loss of ozone under such circumstances.

**Step 5: Evaluate the Answer Choices**

**(A)** would directly back up the scientists' claim, showing a continued depletion of the ozone after we stop production of CFCs.

**(B)** would not help. If these other chemicals were less harmful to the ozone, then there's no support for the idea that the ozone would continue being depleted if CFC production halted.

**(C)** is irrelevant. This is already supported by the passage, but does not strengthen the idea that the ozone layer would still be in trouble if CFC production stopped.

**(D)** is irrelevant. The approval of the scientists' *methods* does nothing to support the *results* they predict.

**(E)** is irrelevant. This suggests that the problem will continue because some countries won't stop producing CFCs. However, it does not support whether the problem would continue if those countries *did* stop.

### 25. (D) Inference

#### Step 2: Identify the Question Type

The question asks for something "strongly supported" by the passage, making this an Inference question.

#### Step 3: Research the Relevant Text

There are no context clues here, so the entire passage is relevant.

#### Step 4: Make a Prediction

With no hints in the question stem, the correct answer could reference anything from anywhere in the passage. In this case, go through the answers one at a time, eliminating those that are clearly wrong. Then, use content clues in the remaining answers to do any necessary research.

#### Step 5: Evaluate the Answer Choices

**(D)** is supported. The regulations are designed to reduce CFC production, thus preserving the ozone layer. This *indirectly* helps with skin cancer rates, as the ozone layer protects us from skin-cancer-producing UV light (lines 1–6).

**(A)** is a Distortion. According to lines 11–13, the ozone layer should be fine in "the absence of pollutants." That would certainly include chlorine, but there could still be plenty of other damaging pollutants if chlorine was not around. Furthermore, lines 13–14 indicate that there is "natural production and destruction of the gas [ozone] over time." So, ozone destruction does naturally occur, but it also naturally regenerates.

**(B)** is Extreme. The first sentence merely says that UV light *contributes* to skin cancer, not that it is the *primary* cause.

**(C)** is Out of Scope. While other chemicals are not mentioned specifically in the passage, there most certainly could be plenty of other such damaging chemicals.

**(E)** is a Distortion. The upward flow of CFCs does not have to be *mainly* over Antarctica. There could be other reasons for the hole appearing there (e.g., the ozone layer is just thinner there).

### 26. (D) Logic Reasoning (Evaluate the Argument)

#### Step 2: Identify the Question Type

The question asks for something that would be "useful in determining" whether something is valid. That makes this an Evaluate the Argument question, similar to those found in Logical Reasoning.

#### Step 3: Research the Relevant Text

The effect of CFCs on the ozone layer is described in detail in paragraph 2.

#### Step 4: Make a Prediction

The question wants an experiment that will test whether a CFC substitute would be safer for the ozone. According to lines 23–25, CFCs themselves are not directly the problem. The problem occurs when they break down into their constituent elements, particularly chlorine. It's the chlorine that reacts with the ozone and destroys it (lines 29–33). So, a good experiment for a CFC substitute would be to make sure that the chemical (or its components) doesn't have the same damaging effect that chlorine has.

#### Step 5: Evaluate the Answer Choices

**(D)** would properly test the replacement. If the chemical or its components were similar to chlorine, they would likely be equally damaging to the ozone. However, if the chemical were completely *unlike* chlorine, there would be one less reason to worry about the ozone.

**(A)** is irrelevant. The whole question is about whether it would affect the ozone layer. Effects on *other* forms of oxygen would not matter at all.

**(B)** would not help. The question is whether it would react with *ozone*, not just any chemicals found in the atmosphere.

**(C)** is a Distortion. The chemical is meant to replace one with chlorine, so the effects on chlorine would have no bearing on how the replacement chemical would affect *ozone*. There's no concern about it *reacting with* chlorine, but there is a concern about the replacement becoming chlorine or chlorine-like and reacting with *ozone*.

**(E)** is a Distortion. The problem is not that CFCs break down into components. The problem is that they break down into *chlorine*. So, if the chemical did not contain chlorine, then it wouldn't matter at all whether the chemical breaks down or not.

### 27. (B) Inference

#### Step 2: Identify the Question Type

The correct answer will be "strongly supported" by the passage, making this an Inference question.

#### Step 3: Research the Relevant Text

With no line references or content clues, the entire text is relevant.

#### Step 4: Make a Prediction

Because of the open-ended nature of the question, it is not worth trying to make an exact prediction. However, a quick glance does show that four answers mention "refrigerant chemicals," which are brought up only in the very last sentence of the passage (line 60). The new ones are called "more environmentally friendly," which at least suggests that newer refrigerant chemicals don't have the same damaging effect on the ozone layer as CFCs do.

### Step 5: Evaluate the Answer Choices

**(B)** is supported by the last sentence, which calls refrigerant chemicals "more environmentally friendly" than CFCs. The whole problem with CFCs is the release of chlorine, so new refrigerant chemicals must not release as much.

**(A)** is Extreme. Just because CFCs were used doesn't mean there was *no* other known refrigerant chemical at the time.

**(C)** is Out of Scope. No information is given for why CFCs were used, let alone whether they were "energy efficient" (or even the *most* energy efficient).

**(D)** is not supported. The Montreal Protocol was an international agreement that came out in 1987 (lines 54–55). CFCs were already banned in North America by the late 1970s (lines 56–57).

**(E)** is also not supported. Refrigerant chemicals are described as "more environmentally friendly" (line 60). While this does not prove that they are entirely free of harmful chemicals, it certainly does not suggest that they are damaging either.

# Glossary

# Logical Reasoning
## Logical Reasoning Question Types

### Argument-Based Questions

#### Main Point Question

A question that asks for an argument's conclusion or an author's main point. Typical question stems:

Which one the following most accurately expresses the conclusion of the argument as a whole?

Which one of the following sentences best expresses the main point of the scientist's argument?

#### Role of a Statement Question

A question that asks how a specific sentence, statement, or idea functions within an argument. Typical question stems:

Which one of the following most accurately describes the role played in the argument by the statement that automation within the steel industry allowed steel mills to produce more steel with fewer workers?

The claim that governmental transparency is a nation's primary defense against public-sector corruption figures in the argument in which one of the following ways?

#### Point at Issue Question

A question that asks you to identify the specific claim, statement, or recommendation about which two speakers/authors disagree (or, rarely, about which they agree). Typical question stems:

A point at issue between Tom and Jerry is

The dialogue most strongly supports the claim that Marilyn and Billy disagree with each other about which one of the following?

#### Method of Argument Question

A question that asks you to describe an author's argumentative strategy. In other words, the correct answer describes *how* the author argues (not necessarily what the author says). Typical question stems:

Which one of the following most accurately describes the technique of reasoning employed by the argument?

Julian's argument proceeds by

In the dialogue, Alexander responds to Abigail in which one of the following ways?

#### Parallel Reasoning Question

A question that asks you to identify the answer choice containing an argument that has the same logical structure and reaches the same type of conclusion as the argument in the stimulus does. Typical question stems:

The pattern of reasoning in which one of the following arguments is most parallel to that in the argument above?

The pattern of reasoning in which one of the following arguments is most similar to the pattern of reasoning in the argument above?

### Assumption-Family Questions

#### Assumption Question

A question that asks you to identify one of the unstated premises in an author's argument. Assumption questions come in two varieties.

**Necessary Assumption** questions ask you to identify an unstated premise required for an argument's conclusion to follow logically from its evidence. Typical question stems:

Which one of the following is an assumption on which the argument depends?

Which one of the following is an assumption that the argument requires in order for its conclusion to be properly drawn?

**Sufficient Assumption** questions ask you to identify an unstated premise sufficient to establish the argument's conclusion on the basis of its evidence. Typical question stems:

The conclusion follows logically if which one of the following is assumed?

Which one of the following, if assumed, enables the conclusion above to be properly inferred?

#### Strengthen/Weaken Question

A question that asks you to identify a fact that, if true, would make the argument's conclusion more likely (Strengthen) or less likely (Weaken) to follow from its evidence. Typical question stems:

#### Strengthen

Which one of the following, if true, most strengthens the argument above?

Which one the following, if true, most strongly supports the claim above?

#### Weaken

Which one of the following, if true, would most weaken the argument above?

Which one of the following, if true, most calls into question the claim above?

#### Flaw Question

A question that asks you to describe the reasoning error that the author has made in an argument. Typical question stems:

The argument's reasoning is most vulnerable to criticism on the grounds that the argument

Which of the following identifies a reasoning error in the argument?

The reasoning in the correspondent's argument is questionable because the argument

### Parallel Flaw Question

A question that asks you to identify the argument that contains the same error(s) in reasoning that the argument in the stimulus contains. Typical question stems:

The pattern of flawed reasoning exhibited by the argument above is most similar to that exhibited in which one of the following?

Which one of the following most closely parallels the questionable reasoning cited above?

### Evaluate the Argument Question

A question that asks you to identify an issue or consideration relevant to the validity of an argument. Think of Evaluate questions as "Strengthen or Weaken" questions. The correct answer, if true, will strengthen the argument, and if false, will weaken the argument, or vice versa. Evaluate questions are very rare. Typical question stems:

Which one of the following would be most useful to know in order to evaluate the legitimacy of the professor's argument?

It would be most important to determine which one of the following in evaluating the argument?

## Non-Argument Questions

### Inference Question

A question that asks you to identify a statement that follows from the statements in the stimulus. It is very important to note the characteristics of the one correct and the four incorrect answers before evaluating the choices in Inference questions. Depending on the wording of the question stem, the correct answer to an Inference question may be the one that

- *must be true* if the statements in the stimulus are true

- is *most strongly supported* by the statements in the stimulus

- *must be false* if the statements in the stimulus are true

Typical question stems:

If all of the statements above are true, then which one of the following must also be true?

Which one of the following can be properly inferred from the information above?

If the statements above are true, then each of the following could be true EXCEPT:

Which one of the following is most strongly supported by the information above?

The statements above, if true, most support which one of the following?

The facts described above provide the strongest evidence against which one of the following?

### Paradox Question

A question that asks you to identify a fact that, if true, most helps to explain, resolve, or reconcile an apparent contradiction. Typical question stems:

Which one of the following, if true, most helps to explain how both studies' findings could be accurate?

Which one the following, if true, most helps to resolve the apparent conflict in the spokesperson's statements?

Each one of the following, if true, would contribute to an explanation of the apparent discrepancy in the information above EXCEPT:

## Principle Questions

### Principle Question

A question that asks you to identify corresponding cases and principles. Some Principle questions provide a principle in the stimulus and call for the answer choice describing a case that corresponds to the principle. Others provide a specific case in the stimulus and call for the answer containing a principle to which that case corresponds.

On the LSAT, Principle questions almost always mirror the skills rewarded by other Logical Reasoning question types. After each of the following Principle question stems, we note the question type it resembles. Typical question stems:

Which one of the following principles, if valid, most helps to justify the reasoning above? (**Strengthen**)

Which one of the following most accurately expresses the principle underlying the reasoning above? (**Assumption**)

The situation described above most closely conforms to which of the following generalizations? (**Inference**)

Which one of the following situations conforms most closely to the principle described above? (**Inference**)

Which one of the following principles, if valid, most helps to reconcile the apparent conflict among the prosecutor's claims? (**Paradox**)

### Parallel Principle Question

A question that asks you to identify a specific case that illustrates the same principle that is illustrated by the case described in the stimulus. Typical question stem:

Of the following, which one illustrates a principle that is most similar to the principle illustrated by the passage?

# Untangling the Stimulus

## Conclusion Types

The conclusions in arguments found in the Logical Reasoning section of the LSAT tend to fall into one of six categories:

1) Value Judgment (an evaluative statement; e.g., Action X is unethical, or Y's recital was poorly sung)

2) "If"/Then (a conditional prediction, recommendation, or assertion; e.g., If X is true, then so is Y, or If you an M, then you should do N)

3) Prediction (X *will* or *will not* happen in the future)

4) Comparison (X is taller/shorter/more common/less common, etc. than Y)

5) Assertion of Fact (X is true or X is false)

6) Recommendation (we *should* or *should not* do X)

## One-Sentence Test

A tactic used to identify the author's conclusion in an argument. Consider which sentence in the argument is the one the author would keep if asked to get rid of everything except her main point.

## Subsidiary Conclusion

A conclusion following from one piece of evidence and then used by the author to support his overall conclusion or main point. Consider the following argument:

> The pharmaceutical company's new experimental treatment did not succeed in clinical trials. As a result, the new treatment will not reach the market this year. Thus, the company will fall short of its revenue forecasts for the year.

Here, the sentence "As a result, the new treatment will not reach the market this year" is a subsidiary conclusion. It follows from the evidence that the new treatment failed in clinical trials, and it provides evidence for the overall conclusion that the company will not meet its revenue projections.

## Keyword(s) in Logical Reasoning

A word or phrase that helps you untangle a question's stimulus by indicating the logical structure of the argument or the author's point. Here are three categories of Keywords to which LSAT experts pay special attention in Logical Reasoning:

**Conclusion** words; e.g., *therefore, thus, so, as a result, it follows that, consequently*, [evidence] *is evidence that* [conclusion]

**Evidence** word; e.g, *because, since, after all, for,* [evidence] *is evidence that* [conclusion]

**Contrast** words; e.g., *but, however, while, despite, in spite of, on the other hand* (These are especially useful in Paradox and Inference questions.)

Experts use Keywords even more extensively in Reading Comprehension. Learn the Keywords associated with the Reading Comprehension section, and apply them to Logical Reasoning when they are helpful.

## Mismatched Concepts

One of two patterns to which authors' assumptions conform in LSAT arguments. Mismatched Concepts describes the assumption in arguments in which terms or concepts in the conclusion are different *in kind* from those in the evidence. The author assumes that there is a logical relationship between the different terms. For example:

> Bobby is a **championship swimmer**. Therefore, he **trains every day**.

Here, the words "trains every day" appear only in the conclusion, and the words "championship swimmer" appear only in the evidence. For the author to reach this conclusion from this evidence, he assumes that championship swimmers train every day.

Another example:

> Susan does **not eat her vegetables**. Thus, she will **not grow big and strong**.

In this argument, not growing big and strong is found only in the conclusion while not eating vegetables is found only in the evidence. For the author to reach this conclusion from this evidence, she must assume that eating one's vegetables is necessary for one to grow big and strong.

See also Overlooked Possibilities.

## Overlooked Possibilities

One of two patterns to which authors' assumptions conform in LSAT arguments. Mismatched Concepts describes the assumption in arguments in which terms or concepts in the conclusion are different *in degree, scale, or level of certainty* from those in the evidence. The author assumes that there is no factor or explanation for the conclusion other than the one(s) offered in the evidence. For example:

> Samson does not have a ticket stub for this movie showing. Thus, Samson must have sneaked into the movie without paying.

The author assumes that there is no other explanation for Samson's lack of a ticket stub. The author overlooks several possibilities: e.g., Samson had a special pass for this showing of the movie; Samson dropped his ticket stub by accident or threw it away after entering the theater; someone else in Samson's party has all of the party members' ticket stubs in her pocket or handbag.

Another example:

> Jonah's marketing plan will save the company money. Therefore, the company should adopt Jonah's plan.

Here, the author makes a recommendation based on one advantage. The author assumes that the advantage is the company's only concern or that there are no disadvantages that could outweigh it, e.g., Jonah's plan might save money on marketing but not generate any new leads or customers; Jonah's plan might damage the company's image or reputation; Jonah's plan might include illegal false advertising. Whenever the author of an LSAT argument concludes with a recommendation or a prediction based on just a single fact in the evidence, that author is always overlooking many other possibilities.

See also Mismatched Concepts.

### Causal Argument

An argument in which the author concludes or assumes that one thing causes another. The most common pattern on the LSAT is for the author to conclude that A causes B from evidence that A and B are correlated. For example:

> I notice that whenever the store has a poor sales month, employee tardiness is also higher that month. Therefore, it must be that employee tardiness causes the store to lose sales.

The author assumes that the correlation in the evidence indicates a causal relationship. These arguments are vulnerable to three types of overlooked possibilities:

1) There could be **another causal factor**. In the previous example, maybe the months in question are those in which the manager takes vacation, causing the store to lose sales and permitting employees to arrive late without fear of the boss's reprimands.

2) Causation could be **reversed**. Maybe in months when sales are down, employee morale suffers and tardiness increases as a result.

3) The correlation could be **coincidental**. Maybe the correlation between tardiness and the dip in sales is pure coincidence.

See also Flaw Types: Correlation versus Causation.

Another pattern in causal arguments (less frequent on the LSAT) involves the assumption that a particular causal mechanism is or is not involved in a causal relationship. For example:

> The airport has rerouted takeoffs and landings so that they will not create noise over the Sunnyside neighborhood. Thus, the recent drop in Sunnyside's property values cannot be explained by the neighborhood's proximity to the airport.

Here, the author assumes that the only way that the airport could be the cause of dropping property values is through noise pollution. The author overlooks any other possible mechanism (e.g., frequent traffic jams and congestion) through which proximity to the airport could be cause of Sunnyside's woes.

### Principle

A broad, law-like rule, definition, or generalization that covers a variety of specific cases with defined attributes. To see how principles are treated on the LSAT, consider the following principle:

> It is immoral for a person for his own gain to mislead another person.

That principle would cover a specific case, such as a seller who lies about the quality of construction to get a higher price for his house. It would also correspond to the case of a teenager who, wishing to spend a night out on the town, tells his mom "I'm going over to Randy's house." He knows that his mom believes that he will be staying at Randy's house, when in fact, he and Randy will go out together.

That principle does not, however, cover cases in which someone lies solely for the purpose of making the other person feel better or in which one person inadvertently misleads the other through a mistake of fact.

Be careful not to apply your personal ethics or morals when analyzing the principles articulated on the test.

## Flaw Types

### Necessary versus Sufficient

This flaw occurs when a speaker or author concludes that one event is necessary for a second event from evidence that the first event is sufficient to bring about the second event, or vice versa. Example:

> If more than 25,000 users attempt to access the new app at the same time, the server will crash. Last night, at 11:15 pm, the server crashed, so it must be case that more than 25,000 users were attempting to use the new app at that time.

In making this argument, the author assumes that the only thing that will cause the server to crash is the usage level (i.e., high usage is *necessary* for the server to crash). The evidence, however, says that high usage is one thing that will cause the server to crash (i.e., that high usage is *sufficient* to crash the server).

### Correlation versus Causation

This flaw occurs when a speaker or author draws a conclusion that one thing causes another from evidence that the two things are correlated. Example:

Over the past half century, global sugar consumption has tripled. That same time period has seen a surge in the rate of technological advancement worldwide. It follows that the increase in sugar consumption has caused the acceleration in technological advancement.

In any argument with this structure, the author is making three unwarranted assumptions. First, he assumes that there is no alternate cause, i.e., there is nothing else that has contributed to rapid technological advancement. Second, he assumes that the causation is not reversed, i.e., technological advancement has not contributed to the increase in sugar consumption, perhaps by making it easier to grow, refine, or transport sugar. And, third, he assumes that the two phenomena are not merely coincidental, i.e., that it is not just happenstance that global sugar consumption is up at the same time that the pace of technological advancement has accelerated.

## Unrepresentative Sample

This flaw occurs when a speaker or author draws a conclusion about a group from evidence in which the sample cannot represent that group because the sample is too small or too selective, or is biased in some way. Example:

> Moviegoers in our town prefer action films and romantic comedies over other film genres. Last Friday, we sent reporters to survey moviegoers at several theaters in town, and nearly 90 percent of those surveyed were going to watch either an action film or a romantic comedy.

The author assumes that the survey was representative of the town's moviegoers, but there are several reasons to question that assumption. First, we don't know how many people were actually surveyed. Even if the number of people surveyed was adequate, we don't know how many other types of movies were playing. Finally, the author doesn't limit her conclusion to moviegoers on Friday nights. If the survey had been conducted at Sunday matinees, maybe most moviegoers would have been heading out to see an animated family film or a historical drama. Who knows?

## Scope Shift/Unwarranted Assumption

This flaw occurs when a speaker's or author's evidence has a scope or has terms different enough from the scope or terms in his conclusion that it is doubtful that the evidence can support the conclusion. Example:

> A very small percentage of working adults in this country can correctly define collateralized debt obligation securities. Thus, sad to say, the majority of the nation's working adults cannot make prudent choices about how to invest their savings.

This speaker assumes that prudent investing requires the ability to accurately define a somewhat obscure financial term. But prudence is not the same thing as expertise, and the speaker does not offer any evidence that this knowledge of this particular term is related to wise investing.

## Percent versus Number/Rate versus Number

This flaw occurs when a speaker or author draws a conclusion about real quantities from evidence about rates or percentages, or vice versa. Example:

> At the end of last season, Camp SunnyDay laid off half of their senior counselors and a quarter of their junior counselors. Thus, Camp SunnyDay must have more senior counselors than junior counselors.

The problem, of course, is that we don't know how many senior and junior counselors were on staff before the layoffs. If there were a total of 4 senior counselors and 20 junior counselors, then the camp would have laid off only 2 senior counselors while dismissing 5 junior counselors.

## Equivocation

This flaw occurs when a speaker or author uses the same word in two different and incompatible ways. Example:

> Our opponent in the race has accused our candidate's staff members of behaving unprofessionally. But that's not fair. Our staff is made up entirely of volunteers, not paid campaign workers.

The speaker interprets the opponent's use of the word *professional* to mean "paid," but the opponent likely meant something more along the lines of "mature, competent, and businesslike."

## Ad Hominem

This flaw occurs when a speaker or author concludes that another person's claim or argument is invalid because that other person has a personal flaw or shortcoming. One common pattern is for the speaker or author to claim the other person acts hypocritically or that the other person's claim is made from self-interest. Example:

> Mrs. Smithers testified before the city council, stating that the speed limits on the residential streets near her home are dangerously high. But why should we give her claim any credence? The way she eats and exercises, she's not even looking out for her own health.

The author attempts to undermine Mrs. Smithers's testimony by attacking her character and habits. He doesn't offer any evidence that is relevant to her claim about speed limits.

## Part versus Whole

This flaw occurs when a speaker or author concludes that a part or individual has a certain characteristic because the whole or the larger group has that characteristic, or vice versa. Example:

> Patient: I should have no problems taking the three drugs prescribed to me by my doctors. I looked them up, and

none of the three is listed as having any major side effects.

Here, the patient is assuming that what is true of each of the drugs individually will be true of them when taken together. The patient's flaw is overlooking possible interactions that could cause problems not present when the drugs are taken separately.

### Circular Reasoning

This flaw occurs when a speaker or author tries to prove a conclusion with evidence that is logically equivalent to the conclusion. Example:

> All those who run for office are prevaricators. To see this, just consider politicians: they all prevaricate.

Perhaps the author has tried to disguise the circular reasoning in this argument by exchanging the words "those who run for office" in the conclusion for "politicians" in the evidence, but all this argument amounts to is "Politicians prevaricate; therefore, politicians prevaricate." On the LSAT, circular reasoning is very rarely the correct answer to a Flaw question, although it is regularly described in one of the wrong answers.

# Question Strategies

### Denial Test

A tactic for identifying the assumption *necessary* to an argument. When you negate an assumption necessary to an argument, the argument will fall apart. Negating an assumption that is not necessary to the argument will not invalidate the argument. Consider the following argument:

> Only high schools which produced a state champion athlete during the school year will be represented at the Governor's awards banquet. Therefore, McMurtry High School will be represented at the Governor's awards banquet.

Which one of the following is an assumption necessary to that argument?

> (1) McMurtry High School produced more state champion athletes than any other high school during the school year.

> (2) McMurtry High School produced at least one state champion athlete during the school year.

If you are at all confused about which of those two statements reflects the *necessary* assumption, negate them both.

> (1) McMurtry High School **did not produce more** state champion athletes than any other high school during the school year.

That does not invalidate the argument. McMurtry could still be represented at the Governor's banquet.

> (2) McMurtry High School **did not produce any** state champion athletes during the school year.

Here, negating the statement causes the argument to fall apart. Statement (2) is an assumption *necessary* to the argument.

### Point at Issue "Decision Tree"

A tactic for evaluating the answer choices in Point at Issue questions. The correct answer is the only answer choice to which you can answer "Yes" to all three questions in the following diagram.

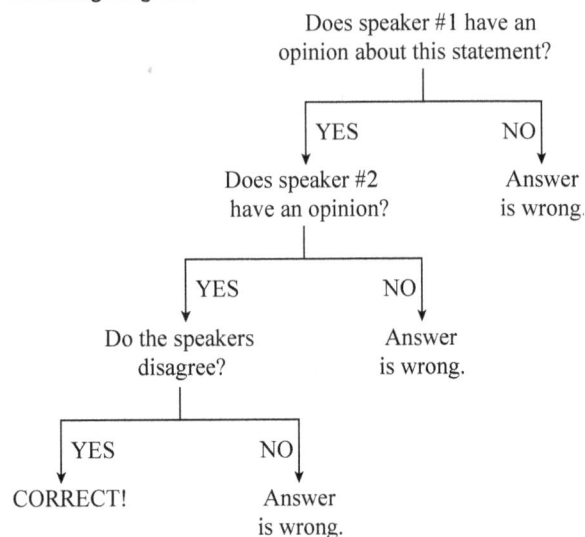

### Common Methods of Argument

These methods of argument or argumentative strategies are common on the LSAT:

- Analogy, in which an author draws parallels between two unrelated (but purportedly similar) situations
- Example, in which an author cites a specific case or cases to justify a generalization
- Counterexample, in which an author seeks to discredit an opponent's argument by citing a specific case or cases that appear to invalidate the opponent's generalization
- Appeal to authority, in which an author cites an expert's claim or opinion as support for her conclusion
- Ad hominem attack, in which an author attacks her opponent's personal credibility rather than attacking the substance of her opponent's argument
- Elimination of alternatives, in which an author lists possibilities and discredits or rules out all but one

- Means/requirements, in which the author argues that something is needed to achieve a desired result

## Wrong Answer Types in LR

### Outside the Scope (Out of Scope; Beyond the Scope)

An answer choice containing a statement that is too broad, too narrow, or beyond the purview of the stimulus, making the statement in the choice irrelevant

### 180

An answer choice that directly contradicts what the correct answer must say (for example, a choice that strengthens the argument in a Weaken question)

### Extreme

An answer choice containing language too emphatic to be supported by the stimulus; often (although not always) characterized by words such as *all*, *never*, *every*, *only*, or *most*

### Distortion

An answer choice that mentions details from the stimulus but mangles or misstates what the author said about those details

### Irrelevant Comparison

An answer choice that compares two items or attributes in a way not germane to the author's argument or statements

### Half-Right/Half-Wrong

An answer choice that begins correctly, but then contradicts or distorts the passage in its second part; this wrong answer type is more common in Reading Comprehension than it is in Logical Reasoning

### Faulty Use of Detail

An answer choice that accurately states something from the stimulus, but does so in a manner that answers the question incorrectly; this wrong answer type is more common in Reading Comprehension than it is in Logical Reasoning

# Logic Games

## Game Types

### Strict Sequencing Game

A game that asks you to arrange entities into numbered positions or into a set schedule (usually hours or days). Strict Sequencing is, by far, the most common game type on the LSAT. In the typical Strict Sequencing game, there is a one-to-one matchup of entities and positions, e.g., seven entities to be placed in seven positions, one per position, or six entities to be placed over six consecutive days, one entity per day.

From time to time, the LSAT will offer Strict Sequencing with more entities than positions (e.g., seven entities to be arranged over five days, with some days to receive more than one entity) or more positions than entities (e.g., six entities to be scheduled over seven days, with at least one day to receive no entities).

Other, less common variations on Strict Sequencing include:

**Double Sequencing**, in which each entity is placed or scheduled two times (there have been rare occurrences of Triple or Quadruple Sequencing). Alternatively, a Double Sequencing game may involve two different sets of entities each sequenced once.

**Circular Sequencing**, in which entities are arranged around a table or in a circular arrangement (NOTE: When the positions in a Circular Sequencing game are numbered, the first and last positions are adjacent.)

**Vertical Sequencing**, in which the positions are numbered from top to bottom or from bottom to top (as in the floors of a building)

### Loose Sequencing Game

A game that asks you to arrange or schedule entities in order but provides no numbering or naming of the positions. The rules in Loose Sequencing give only the relative positions (earlier or later, higher or lower) between two entities or among three entities. Loose Sequencing games almost always provide that there will be no ties between entities in the rank, order, or position they take.

### Circular Sequencing Game

See Strict Sequencing Game.

### Selection Game

A game that asks you to choose or include some entities from the initial list of entities and to reject or exclude others. Some Selection games provide overall limitations on the number of entities to be selected (e.g., "choose exactly four of seven students" or "choose at least two of six entrees") while others provide little or no restriction on the number selected ("choose at least one type of flower" or "select from among seven board members").

### Distribution Game

A game that asks you to break up the initial list of entities into two, three, or (very rarely) four groups or teams. In the vast majority of Distribution games, each entity is assigned to one and only one group or team. A relatively common variation on Distribution games will provide a subdivided list of entities (e.g., eight students—four men and four women—will form three study groups) and will then require representatives from those subdivisions on each team (e.g., each study group will have at least one of the men on it).

### Matching Game

A game that asks you to match one or more members of one set of entities to specific members of another set of entities, or that asks you to match attributes or objects to a set of entities. Unlike Distribution games, in which each entity is placed in exactly one group or team, Matching games usually permit you to assign the same attribute or object to more than one entity.

In some cases, there are overall limitations on the number of entities that can be matched (e.g., "In a school's wood shop, there are four workstations—numbered 1 through 4—and each workstation has at least one and at most three of the following tools—band saw, dremmel tool, electric sander, and power drill"). In almost all Matching games, further restrictions on the number of entities that can be matched to a particular person or place will be found in the rules (e.g., Workstation 4 will have more tools than Workstation 2 has).

### Hybrid Game

A game that asks you to do two (or rarely, three) of the standard actions (Sequencing, Selection, Distribution, and Matching) to a set of entities.

The most common Hybrid is Sequencing-Matching. A typical Sequencing-Matching Hybrid game might ask you to schedule six speakers at a conference to six one-hour speaking slots (from 9 am to 2 pm), and then assign each speaker one of two subjects (economic development or trade policy).

Nearly as common as Sequencing-Matching is Distribution-Sequencing. A typical game of this type might ask you to divide six people in a talent competition into either a Dance category or a Singing category, and then rank the competitors in each category.

It is most common to see one Hybrid game in each Logic Games section, although there have been tests with two Hybrid games and tests with none. To determine the type of Hybrid you are faced with, identify the game's action in Step 1 of the Logic Games Method. For example, a game asking you to choose four of six runners, and then assign the four chosen runners to lanes numbered 1 through 4 on a track, would be a Selection-Sequencing Hybrid game.

### Mapping Game

A game that provides you with a description of geographical locations and, typically, of the connections among them. Mapping games often ask you to determine the shortest possible routes between two locations or to account for the number of connections required to travel from one location to another. This game type is extremely rare, and as of February 2017, a Mapping game was last seen on PrepTest 40 administered in June 2003.

### Process Game

A game that opens with an initial arrangement of entities (e.g., a starting sequence or grouping) and provides rules that describe the processes through which that arrangement can be altered. The questions typically ask you for acceptable arrangements or placements of particular entities after one, two, or three stages in the process. Occasionally, a Process game question might provide information about the arrangement after one, two, or three stages in the process and ask you what must have happened in the earlier stages. This game type is extremely rare, and as of November 2016, a Process game was last seen on PrepTest 16 administered in September 1995. However, there was a Process game on PrepTest 80, administered in December 2016, thus ending a 20-year hiatus.

## Game Setups and Deductions

### Floater

An entity that is not restricted by any rule or limitation in the game

### Blocks of Entities

Two or more entities that are required by rule to be adjacent or separated by a set number of spaces (Sequencing games), to be placed together in the same group (Distribution games), to be matched to the same entity (Matching games), or to be selected or rejected together (Selection games)

### Limited Options

Rules or restrictions that force all of a game's acceptable arrangements into two (or occasionally three) patterns

### Established Entities

An entity required by rule to be placed in one space or assigned to one particular group throughout the entire game

### Number Restrictions

Rules or limitations affecting the number of entities that may be placed into a group or space throughout the game

### Duplications

Two or more rules that restrict a common entity. Usually, these rules can be combined to reach additional deductions. For example, if you know that B is placed earlier than A in a sequence and that C is placed earlier than B in that sequence, you can deduce that C is placed earlier than A in the sequence and that there is at least one space (the space occupied by B) between C and A.

### Master Sketch

The final sketch derived from the game's setup, rules, and deductions. LSAT experts preserve the Master Sketch for reference as they work through the questions. The Master

Sketch does not include any conditions from New-"If" question stems.

## Logic Games Question Types

### Acceptability Question

A question in which the correct answer is an acceptable arrangement of all the entities relative to the spaces, groups, or selection criteria in the game. Answer these by using the rules to eliminate answer choices that violate the rules.

### Partial Acceptability Question

A question in which the correct answer is an acceptable arrangement of some of the entities relative to some of the spaces, groups, or selection criteria in the game, and in which the arrangement of entities not included in the answer choices could be acceptable to the spaces, groups, or selection criteria not explicitly shown in the answer choices. Answer these the same way you would answer Acceptability questions, by using the rules to eliminate answer choices that explicitly or implicitly violate the rules.

### Must Be True/False; Could Be True/False Question

A question in which the correct answer must be true, could be true, could be false, or must be false (depending on the question stem), and in which no additional rules or conditions are provided by the question stem

### New-"If" Question

A question in which the stem provides an additional rule, condition, or restriction (applicable only to that question), and then asks what must/could be true/false as a result. LSAT experts typically handle New-"If" questions by copying the Master Sketch, adding the new restriction to the copy, and working out any additional deductions available as a result of the new restriction before evaluating the answer choices.

### Rule Substitution Question

A question in which the correct answer is a rule that would have an impact identical to one of the game's original rules on the entities in the game

### Rule Change Question

A question in which the stem alters one of the original rules in the game, and then asks what must/could be true/false as a result. LSAT experts typically handle Rule Change questions by reconstructing the game's sketch, but now accounting for the changed rule in place of the original. These questions are rare on recent tests.

### Rule Suspension Question

A question in which the stem indicates that you should ignore one of the original rules in the game, and then asks what must/could be true/false as a result. LSAT experts typically handle Rule Suspension questions by reconstructing

the game's sketch, but now accounting for the absent rule. These questions are very rare.

### Complete and Accurate List Question

A question in which the correct answer is a list of any and all entities that could acceptably appear in a particular space or group, or a list of any and all spaces or groups in which a particular entity could appear

### Completely Determine Question

A question in which the correct answer is a condition that would result in exactly one acceptable arrangement for all of the entities in the game

### Supply the "If" Question

A question in which the correct answer is a condition that would guarantee a particular result stipulated in the question stem

### Minimum/Maximum Question

A question in which the correct answer is the number corresponding to the fewest or greatest number of entities that could be selected (Selection), placed into a particular group (Distribution), or matched to a particular entity (Matching). Often, Minimum/Maximum questions begin with New-"If" conditions.

### Earliest/Latest Question

A question in which the correct answer is the earliest or latest position in which an entity may acceptably be placed. Often, Earliest/Latest questions begin with New-"If" conditions.

### "How Many" Question

A question in which the correct answer is the exact number of entities that may acceptably be placed into a particular group or space. Often, "How Many" questions begin with New-"If" conditions.

# Reading Comprehension
## Strategic Reading

### Roadmap

The test taker's markup of the passage text in Step 1 (Read the Passage Strategically) of the Reading Comprehension Method. To create helpful Roadmaps, LSAT experts circle or underline Keywords in the passage text and jot down brief, helpful notes or paragraph summaries in the margin of their test booklets.

### Keyword(s) in Reading Comprehension

Words in the passage text that reveal the passage structure or the author's point of view and thus help test takers anticipate and research the questions that accompany the passage. LSAT experts pay attention to six categories of Keywords in Reading Comprehension:

**Emphasis/Opinion**—words that signal that the author finds a detail noteworthy or that the author has positive or negative opinion about a detail; any subjective or evaluative language on the author's part (e.g., *especially, crucial, unfortunately, disappointing, I suggest, it seems likely*)

**Contrast**—words indicating that the author finds two details or ideas incompatible or that the two details illustrate conflicting points (e.g., *but, yet, despite, on the other hand*)

**Logic**—words that indicate an argument, either the author's or someone else's (e.g., *thus, therefore, because, it follows that*)

**Illustration**—words indicating an example offered to clarify or support another point (e.g., *for example, this shows, to illustrate*)

**Sequence/Chronology**—words showing steps in a process or developments over time (e.g., *traditionally, in the past, today, first, second, finally, earlier, subsequent*)

**Continuation**—words indicating that a subsequent example or detail supports the same point or illustrates the same idea as the previous example (e.g., *moreover, in addition, also, further, along the same lines*)

### Margin Notes

The brief notes or paragraph summaries that the test taker jots down next to the passage in the margin of the test booklet

### Big Picture Summaries: Topic/Scope/Purpose/Main Idea

A test taker's mental summary of the passage as a whole made during Step 1 (Read the Passage Strategically) of the Reading Comprehension Method. LSAT experts account for four aspects of the passage in their big picture summaries:

**Topic**—the overall subject of the passage

**Scope**—the particular aspect of the Topic that the author focuses on

**Purpose**—the author's reason or motive for writing the passage (express this as a verb; e.g., *to refute, to outline, to evaluate, to critique*)

**Main Idea**—the author's conclusion or overall takeaway; if the passage does not contain an explicit conclusion or thesis, you can combine the author's Scope and Purpose to get a good sense of the Main Idea.

### Passage Types

Kaplan categorizes Reading Comprehension passages in two ways, by subject matter and by passage structure.

*Subject matter categories*

In the majority of LSAT Reading Comprehension sections, there is one passage from each of the following subject matter categories:

**Humanities**—topics from art, music, literature, philosophy, etc.

**Natural Science**—topics from biology, astronomy, paleontology, physics, etc.

**Social Science**—topics from anthropology, history, sociology, psychology, etc.

**Law**—topics from constitutional law, international law, legal education, jurisprudence, etc.

*Passage structure categories*

The majority of LSAT Reading Comprehension passages correspond to one of the following descriptions. The first categories—Theory/Perspective and Event/Phenomenon—have been the most common on recent LSATs.

**Theory/Perspective**—The passage focuses on a thinker's theory or perspective on some aspect of the Topic; typically (though not always), the author disagrees and critiques the thinker's perspective and/or defends his own perspective.

**Event/Phenomenon**—The passage focuses on an event, a breakthrough development, or a problem that has recently arisen; when a solution to the problem is proposed, the author most often agrees with the solution (and that represents the passage's Main Idea).

**Biography**—The passage discusses something about a notable person; the aspect of the person's life emphasized by the author reflects the Scope of the passage.

**Debate**—The passage outlines two opposing positions (neither of which is the author's) on some aspect of the Topic; the author may side with one of the positions, may remain neutral, or may critique both. (This structure has been relatively rare on recent LSATs.)

### Comparative Reading

A pair of passages (labeled Passage A and Passage B) that stand in place of the typical single passage exactly one time in each Reading Comprehension section administered since June 2007. The paired Comparative Reading passages share the same Topic, but may have different Scopes and Purposes. On most LSAT tests, a majority of the questions accompanying Comparative Reading passages require the test taker to compare or contrast ideas or details from both passages.

## Question Strategies

### Research Clues

A reference in a Reading Comprehension question stem to a word, phrase, or detail in the passage text, or to a particular line number or paragraph in the passage. LSAT experts recognize five kinds of research clues:

**Line Reference**—An LSAT expert researches around the referenced lines, looking for Keywords that indicate why the referenced details were included or how they were used by the author.

**Paragraph Reference**—An LSAT expert consults her passage Roadmap to see the paragraph's Scope and Purpose.

**Quoted Text** (often accompanied by a line reference)—An LSAT expert checks the context of the quoted term or phrase, asking what the author meant by it in the passage.

**Proper Nouns**—An LSAT expert checks the context of the person, place, or thing in the passage, asking whether the author made a positive, negative, or neutral evaluation of it and why the author included it in the passage.

**Content Clues**—These are terms, concepts, or ideas from the passage mentioned in the question stem but not as direct quotes and not accompanied by line references. An LSAT expert knows that content clues almost always refer to something that the author emphasized or about which the author expressed an opinion.

## Reading Comp Question Types

### Global Question

A question that asks for the Main Idea of the passage or for the author's primary Purpose in writing the passage. Typical question stems:

> Which one of the following most accurately expresses the main point of the passage?

> The primary purpose of the passage is to

### Detail Question

A question that asks what the passage explicitly states about a detail. Typical question stems:

> According to the passage, some critics have criticized Gilliam's films on the grounds that

> The passage states that one role of a municipality's comptroller in budget decisions by the city council is to

> The author identifies which one of the following as a commonly held but false preconception?

> The passage contains sufficient information to answer which of the following questions?

Occasionally, the test will ask for a correct answer that contains a detail *not* stated in the passage:

> The author attributes each of the following positions to the Federalists EXCEPT:

### Inference Question

A question that asks for a statement that follows from or is based on the passage but that is not necessarily stated explicitly in the passage. Some Inference questions contain research clues. The following are typical Inference question stems containing research clues:

> Based on the passage, the author would be most likely to agree with which one of the following statements about unified field theory?

> The passage suggests which one of the following about the behavior of migratory water fowl?

> Given the information in the passage, to which one of the following would radiocarbon dating techniques likely be applicable?

Other Inference questions lack research clues in the question stem. They may be evaluated using the test taker's Big Picture Summaries, or the answer choices may make it clear that the test taker should research a particular part of the passage text. The following are typical Inference question stems containing research clues:

> It can be inferred from the passage that the author would be most likely to agree that

> Which one of the following statements is most strongly supported by the passage?

Other Reading Comprehension question types categorized as Inference questions are Author's Attitude questions and Vocabulary-in-Context questions.

### Logic Function Question

A question that asks why the author included a particular detail or reference in the passage or how the author used a particular detail or reference. Typical question stems:

> The author of the passage mentions declining inner-city populations in the paragraph most likely in order to

> The author's discussion of Rimbaud's travels in the Mediterranean (lines 23–28) functions primarily to

> Which one of the following best expresses the function of the third paragraph in the passage?

### Logic Reasoning Question

A question that asks the test taker to apply Logical Reasoning skills in relation to a Reading Comprehension passage. Logic Reasoning questions often mirror Strengthen or Parallel Reasoning questions, and occasionally mirror Method of Argument or Principle questions. Typical question stems:

> Which one of the following, if true, would most strengthen the claim made by the author in the last sentence of the passage (lines 51–55)?

> Which one of the following pairs of proposals is most closely analogous to the pair of studies discussed in the passage?

### Author's Attitude Question

A question that asks for the author's opinion or point of view on the subject discussed in the passage or on a detail mentioned in the passage. Since the correct answer may follow from the passage without being explicitly stated in it, some Author's Attitude questions are characterized as a subset of Inference questions. Typical question stems:

> The author's attitude toward the use of DNA evidence in the appeals by convicted felons is most accurately described as

> The author's stance regarding monetarist economic theories can most accurately be described as one of

### Vocabulary-in-Context Question

A question that asks how the author uses a word or phrase within the context of the passage. The word or phrase in question is always one with multiple meanings. Since the correct answer follows from its use in the passage, Vocabulary-in-Context questions are characterized as a subset of Inference questions. Typical question stems:

> Which one of the following is closest in meaning to the word "citation" as it used in the second paragraph of the passage (line 18)?

> In context, the word "enlightenment" (line 24) refers to

## Wrong Answer Types in RC

### Outside the Scope (Out of Scope; Beyond the Scope)

An answer choice containing a statement that is too broad, too narrow, or beyond the purview of the passage

### 180

An answer choice that directly contradicts what the correct answer must say

### Extreme

An answer choice containing language too emphatic (e.g., *all, never, every, none*) to be supported by the passage

### Distortion

An answer choice that mentions details or ideas from the passage but mangles or misstates what the author said about those details or ideas

### Faulty Use of Detail

An answer choice that accurately states something from the passage but in a manner that incorrectly answers the question

### Half-Right/Half-Wrong

An answer choice in which one clause follows from the passage while another clause contradicts or deviates from the passage

# Formal Logic Terms

### Conditional Statement ("If"-Then Statement)

A statement containing a sufficient clause and a necessary clause. Conditional statements can be described in Formal Logic shorthand as:

> If [sufficient clause]   → [necessary clause]

In some explanations, the LSAT expert may refer to the sufficient clause as the statement's "trigger" and to the necessary clause as the statement's result.

For more on how to interpret, describe, and use conditional statements on the LSAT, please refer to "A Note About Formal Logic on the LSAT" in this book's introduction.

### Contrapositive

The conditional statement logically equivalent to another conditional statement formed by reversing the order of and negating the terms in the original conditional statement. For example, reversing and negating the terms in this statement:

> *If     A                    →        B*

results in its contrapositive:

> *If     ~ B                  →        ~ A*

To form the contrapositive of conditional statements in which either the sufficient clause or the necessary clause has more than one term, you must also change the conjunction *and* to *or*, or vice versa. For example, reversing and negating the terms and changing *and* to *or* in this statement:

> *If     M                    →        O AND P*

results in its contrapositive:

> *If     ~ O OR ~ P          →        ~ M*